FREEFALLING

FREEFALLING

WRITING WITHOUT LIMITS

Bernie DeHut
Karen Marie Duquette
L. Marie Elsey
Lori Goff
Maryhelen Hagood
Susan Kehoe
Margo LaGattuta
Dinah Lee
Polly Opsahl
Bob Simion
Mary Simion
Mary Ellen Soroka

Edited by Margo LaGattuta   6/12/07

Best wishes,
Margo LaGattuta
Keep writing!

iUniverse, Inc.
New York Lincoln Shanghai

Freefalling
Writing without Limits

Copyright © 2007 by Margo LaGattuta

iUniverse books may be ordered through booksellers or by contacting:

iUniverse
2021 Pine Lake Road, Suite 100
Lincoln, NE 68512
www.iuniverse.com
1-800-Authors (1-800-288-4677)

The views expressed in this work are solely those of the author and do not necessarily reflect the views of the publisher, and the publisher hereby disclaims any responsibility for them.

Cover design by Tommy Herrmann

ISBN-13: 978-0-595-42727-7 (pbk)
ISBN-13: 978-0-595-87058-5 (ebk)
ISBN-10: 0-595-42727-8 (pbk)
ISBN-10: 0-595-87058-9 (ebk)

Printed in the United States of America

There is no royal path to good writing, and such paths as do exist do not lead through neat critical gardens, various as they are, but through the jungles of self, the world, and of craft.

~Jessamyn West, *Saturday Review,*
21 September 1957

CONTENTS

BLUE CANARY 93
Polly Opsahl

WHAT THE DIRT AND I REMEMBER 113
Bernie DeHut

ACKNOWLEDGMENTS

The following works have been previously published:

Trusting the Lake, Margo LaGattuta, in *Embracing the Fall* (Plain View Press 1994)

What To Do after the Rejection, Margo LaGattuta, in *Wind Eyes* anthology (Plain View Press 1997)

The Cat Waits, Polly Opsahl, *Telling Our Own Stories* (Detroit Worker-Writer Festival 1999)

Gone, Polly Opsahl, in *Encore* (National Federation of State Poetry Societies anthology 2001)

Curtains, Mary Simion, 1st Place winner, Writer's Voice YMCA of Metropolitan Detroit, 2003

Dancing in Time, Mary Simion, Commendation, Springfed Arts: Metro Detroit Writers Poetry and Prose Contest, 2005

Mountain Woman, Lori Goff, in *The Heart of It All* (iUniverse 2006)

INTRODUCTION

MAKE A GOOD STORY
FROM THE GREATER PART OF MEMORY

Margo LaGattuta

I think of years ago when I was a child who loved stories. I remember sitting around the kitchen table and hearing grownups tell tales of their own lives when they were young—the time my father said his brother made him eat a worm. He never forgot it and told the story then with the same squeamishness he must have felt on that foggy summer morning when he lived on a farm in Worcester, Massachusetts. I remember my mother telling how she had to take the trolley car home from school one day when she was sick and how, when she met my father's mother for the first time, my grandmother said she approved of this strange woman for her son's wife because she wore "sensible shoes." I remember playing Toni dolls in the backyard on Hartwell Street with my best friend, Lynne, how we made stylish dresses for them out of silk scarves.

And so the story goes, back and back and back—into a dream of story so old I'm never sure if the incident really happened or I made it up, or someone else made it up and told it to me. Little did I know then that all those images would be stored away in a memory bank to be called up on the page one day in some future life. I certainly didn't know then that any strangers would care to hear about my stories or read them.

That's an amazing thing about the ancient art of storytelling and poem-making that never seems to grow old. We love to hear other people's stories, and something strange happens in the retelling. Each bit of someone else's story can remind us of our own. When Bonnie tells me that her mother in a nursing home is refusing to eat, I think of my own mother in her last month, who had to drink Ensure because she wouldn't eat the establishment's food, yet on her trip home for the weekend, she made me stop at her favorite Dairy Queen for a chili dog topped with hot mustard and onions. She gobbled it down with delight. When anyone shares a memory, we tend to associate and weave our own memory in, so that all of our stories seem to become connected with an invisible silver thread.

I've believed for a long time now, since I began teaching writing workshops, that everyone has a story to tell and needs a safe place to tell it. I've watched people open up and pour out stories and poems that have been stored whole in a memory treasure chest—then blink and wonder where they ever found the words. One student told a memory of when his brother drowned in front of his own eyes, and he couldn't save him. No one in the family was allowed to discuss it for the past ten years, so he kept that difficult story hidden. When it came up through the keys of his computer, it was complete and a great epiphany of long withheld feelings. A bit of grace.

• • •

Freefalling—Writing without Limits is a collection of stories and poems gathered by a group of writers who met in my creative writing workshops. I selected them based on the quality of their work, and we came together twice a month for a year to create this anthology. Our purpose is to share our stories and our process with readers. We believe that many readers are also potential writers who may be able to benefit from learning about the many ways in which we find inspiration. It is our hope to make this a permission-giving book and offer it to you for your own enjoyment and motivation.

We selected the title, *Freefalling—Writing without Limits,* after thinking about how difficult it can be to get started on a creative project. There are so many ways we limit ourselves. Some of us worry about what others may think of what we write, whether we have edited and structured the work well enough, whether we have revealed too much or too little, whether we might hurt someone's feelings by what we say. All of these thoughts are important and can come later in the necessary editing process, but they are by their very nature deadly in the opening stages of writing. We want to suggest that you begin your writing by creating a free space on the page, where you can say whatever you want. Write whatever pops into your head, with no worry about what anyone may think of it, knowing you can revise later, or even toss it away if you wish. Give yourself permission to tell your truth.

Freefalling may have many meanings, and the one we like has to do with parachuting. It's the buoyant freedom of using our natural weight to float before opening the parachute. It's our ability to trust the universe to keep us up. It's getting motivated and having the rush of beautiful scenery to observe before pulling the cord and having a more limiting experience, which includes the steps of editing and finishing. Those are also important steps and necessary for publishing. Without opening our parachute, we hit the ground hard, and that's no fun.

Looking at my years of teaching writing courses, I realize that this freefalling experience is what most people need permission to have. They are used to the judgment experience. They've had it all their lives in school, in business and from English teachers, who are more than happy to stop their freefall and shape their writing up, fix those commas and verb tenses once and for all (sigh). But I spend a lot of time at the beginning of every writing course talking about "doing the dumb one"—free-writing the version that has mistakes but contains the passion of experience. William Stafford said, "I never get writers' block; I just lower my standards." And he meant that getting started we need to undo those judgments (our own and others') that stop us before we scrawl something good on the page. Later we can apply all those important standards. Near the end of every course or workshop, I have writers tell me that was the most important thing I gave them all semester— in effect, the freefalling experience of allowing their words to say whatever they wish before the more left-brained editing process takes over.

We incorporate a *Try this* element in each writer's section, to give you insight into his or her process and offer writing prompts for you to try. At the end of the book, in addition to short biographies of the writers, we include a section with more *Try this* prompts and questions to inspire you to get started on your own writing project. We also include some craft and revision suggestions for writing poetry and stories.

Try this:

Find a picture of yourself as a child and free-write your thoughts as you look at the picture. What is in your mind at this age? What happens just before the photo is snapped—or just after? How does this child turn into the person you are today? Also try this experiment with other old photos from your family album. Who are these people? Especially the ones you've never met. Invent their lives. Speak in the voice of a great aunt who died before you were born or that of a great, great grandfather who has your nose. Now turn these notes into a story or poem. Here is a poem of mine that came from this exercise.

TRUSTING THE LAKE

She floats, her eyes above water, in a black inner tube.
It will hold me up, she thinks. A ten-year-old girl
floating in Lake Manchog is hugging the air.
Waves roll by; she has no idea what's ahead,

but she likes the lightness of clear water.
Even the rain tickles her round face.
She has already caught a glimpse into time,
not all the particulars, but the pattern of things
to come. There are joys ahead, she can hardly

wait for them, but the sorrows are dark pollywogs
hiding like the marshy roots in a nearby bog.
If she knew them all, she'd spring a leak,
jump overboard and sink into the lost palace,

but the camera has a way of keeping her innocent,
expectancy and hope in her near-sighted eyes.
Her hair, parted in the middle, is drawn
back into braids woven together like the two
sides of herself, grief and ecstasy a blend
of inner parts wound round and round, then
bound with a silver elastic knot at the end.

We leave her there floating in an old photo
album. She is suspended forever in that young
moment, that hopeful buoyant pose on the lake.
It will take her years to get it back,
that way of trusting the waves to hold her,
of trusting her own delicate, inner luck.

● ● ●

   Take this powerful chance. Select a notebook or a journal and start to
store your own stories and poems. Make them sad or poignant or silly or
strange. Fill them with blessings you can never forget. Beware, this could take
a lifetime and could make you cry, but it will open up the rooms in your
mind for a new glance—and another new tale to tell.

Margo LaGattuta poet,
essayist, editor

WAITING FOR THE DEER

L. Marie Elsey

Writing memoir is like stripping away layers of old wallpaper. I search for seams that have dried and separated, and when I find one, I pull—ripping a piece of wallpaper until it grows wider and wider, then narrows down to nothing before detaching itself from the wall. But underneath, where it's the widest, a story is exposed. I take this precious tidbit from the past and weave a new story around it. Each time I uncover a memory, I'm delighted all over again at how well the past and the present complement each other. After writing her *Little House on the Prairie* books, Laura Ingalls Wilder is quoted as saying, "When you write about the people you love, they live forever."

Try this:

In *A Celebration of the Bugflies,* sharing fireflies for the first time with my three-year-old grandson, Joshua, uncovered a forgotten memory. Over his cries of "Grandma, Grandma, look there's one," I recalled the laughter of my own grandparents again and wrote a story about the fireflies I had shared with them as a child on their farm in Kentucky. Bringing together on the same page two generations separated by more than fifty years felt like I had defied death and helped them to touch each other for the first time. Strip away the layers of old wallpaper and expose that story underneath. Knit those memories into your everyday experiences and allow the people you love to live forever.

LIVING THE DREAM

for my niece who showed me dreams never die

As a kid I had a direct line to the great American game of baseball because I was born the same year Babe Ruth died. I was confident the skill "The Babe" possessed for the game he played with such fervor had been passed to me. I filled cigar boxes with baseball cards and carefully bent the brim of a baseball cap into a tight arc, creating a kind of baseball tunnel vision when I pulled it low over my eyes on the pitcher's mound. At night I stored a hardball inside my glove, working to form the perfect mitt even while I slept.

So it was with great disappointment when I learned at the age of eight that I would never play major league baseball. Some informed individual was kind enough to fill me in, "You can't play baseball in the big leagues; you're a girl!"

Being a girl had not entered into my equation until that moment. Sure I wore a dress to school, but it didn't hamper my pitching arm. I swung a bat as fiercely as anyone in long pants. Standing side by side on the playground with the other ballplayers, I saw no difference in our demeanor. I was wounded by a world that would squash a girl's dream of taking her love of baseball all the way to Yankee Stadium, the house that Ruth built.

But that was 1956.

Being a girl was not a problem for my niece, Liz, when she played catcher on an all boys' hardball team in 1995. From home plate, she was in command of the team, signaling how many outs and where the next play should be. Her long blond hair didn't surprise anyone in the stands when she slid her catcher's mask off before catching a pop-up or throwing out a runner. Sitting in the bleachers, I listened to the parents discuss Liz's remarkable talents. They viewed her not as an exceptional girl playing a boys' game, but as an exceptional baseball player.

Liz played a left-handed shortstop on the girls' softball team at Rochester High School. She had the coordination to field the ball then twist her body quickly around and set up for the difficult left-handed throw to first base. I marveled at her technique to field ball after ball without a wasted step. When it was Liz's turn at bat, there was always joy in Mudville; mighty Liz rarely struck out.

The house that Ruth built is still a "men's only club." But when I pull my old baseball glove from the shelf in the closet, my dreams still come with it … *From the pitcher's mound inside Yankee Stadium, a baseball cap pulled low over my eyes, I lean forward and concentrate by way of baseball tunnel vision on signals from the catcher. Turning the ball slowly in my hand, searching for the right feel, I keep watch on the runner leading off at first as the batter practice swings. Then, like a fine-tuned engine when the key is turned, everything comes together. I nod to the catcher, straighten up and take a quick glance toward first. The catcher braces as I slingshot the ball toward home plate. The batter begins his swing and the runner leaves first base heading for second.*

After 1956, there was always an ache whenever I thought of my dream to break the sex barrier and take a place beside the other baseball legends of the day. Like Jackie Robinson, I wanted to be a pioneer blazing a trail to another of baseball's finest moments.

Sticking my glove back on the shelf, I wondered if letting women play in the big leagues would have changed the great American game too much. Some traditions were never meant for change.

Liz was voted one of the top 25 female basketball players in Oakland County during her junior and senior years at Rochester High School. She traded her baseball glove for a basketball jersey and a scholarship to Indiana University. Only 5'5", she's as good with a basketball as she was with a baseball. As a point guard she averages over 10 points a game for the Titan Athletics. Liz will graduate next year with a degree in elementary education and the satisfaction of knowing she played four years of terrific women's basketball.

Liz is living the dream.

MISS VANALSTINE'S 4th GRADE LEARNING EXTRAVAGANZA

During Miss Vanalstine's tenure as a teacher, she rarely spared the rod to spoil the child. In the over-crowded classrooms of the 1950's, she navigated sideways down narrow aisles and kept thirty or more students under control with her thunderous voice while she frequently whacked home principles of good behavior with an ancient ruler. Her eccentric nature, coupled with a flair for the dramatic, enhanced her teaching style and motivated even the most troubled student.

Bounced from one school to another, barely able to read, I entered Franklin Elementary School in Royal Oak, Michigan, in March of 1958. I settled nervously into a front row seat at Miss Vanalstine's 4th grade learning extravaganza.

This flamboyant woman fascinated me on the first day when she stood on one foot, jumped up and down, demonstrating a technique for removing water from her ear. At Easter we made bunnies out of thread spools and cotton balls and, if we whispered during a spelling bee, she threw erasers at us from across the room. She told us to be careful with the big paper cutter because it roared like a lion when it chopped down on paper.

Her classroom was filled with books, and several times each month she rotated students, allowing them a fresh view of all the available reading materials. In the late afternoon, when we were tired and sweaty from the playground and comatose in our seats, Miss Vanalstine read aloud stories about a spider named Charlotte and a farmer boy called Almanzo Wilder who grew up long ago.

Miss Vanalstine never married and spent her summers traveling. In class she loved to wave her arms dramatically, then reach up and pull down the world map like a window shade over the blackboard and point excitedly to some far-off country. In the three months I spent in her class, I traveled thousands of miles and never left my desk. She understood ten-year-olds and told her stories accordingly. My worried demeanor began to fade as I listened to her describe the colorful and regimented changing of the guard at Buckingham Palace, the spectacular view of Paris from the Eiffel Tower or what fun it would be to live in Venice and take a gondola to school each day. She painted dreamy pictures with words and hypnotized me with my own imagination.

Three months passed quickly, and when June came, Miss Vanalstine recommended I repeat the fourth grade. My parents decided the stigma connected with failing was too great and, with a kiss on my forehead, Miss Vanalstine reluctantly passed me on.

I believe she spared the rod on many troubled children that came through her classroom in the forty years she taught at Franklin School because I never felt the sting of her ruler. She had found a firm but loving balance for teaching.

I saw Miss Vanalstine years later when I was in college working with a group of students petitioning for stricter gun laws in the city of Royal Oak. When I knocked on the front door of her small one-story brick home on Mohawk Street, located only a few houses from Franklin School, she recognized me and stepped out on the porch. The years fell away as she read my petition and signed her name. In her presence I was ten years old again, daydreaming to stories of faraway places, discovering my potential among her books and maps, thriving in school for the first time in an over-crowded classroom of fourth-graders and one very remarkable teacher.

I heard someone say recently, "In a hundred years the monetary value of your home or car won't matter, but the value of a child is priceless."

I thought of Miss Vanalstine.

THE SECRET OF LIFE

for Elizabeth, Rollin, Joshua, Liam and Morgan

Curly, the gristly weather-beaten cowboy with the gravel voice and a cigarette dangling from his mouth in the movie, *City Slickers*, has a simple philosophy. "The secret of life is one thing, just one thing," he says. "You stick to that and everything else don't mean shit." If asked what that one thing is, Curly rolls his cigarette around on his lips, tilts his head back and through a cloud of smoke he says with a cocky smirk, "That's what you've got to figure out."

Elizabeth watches me put on lipstick, blot my lips with a Kleenex, then tuck the tissue in my purse.

"Grandma, do you know what you did?"

Puzzled, I look down at my granddaughter. "No, what?"

"You put a kiss in your purse."

I remember when Elizabeth was born and how strange it was to hang her baby clothes in the same closet where my business suits had been. I was alert to the newborn sounds that sent me running to her side during evenings when my daughter, Lisa, worked late.

Lisa was in her last semester at Oakland Community College and accepted at Wayne State University when she became pregnant. This unplanned pregnancy could have taken a different turn, but standing in the bathroom and looking at my only granddaughter, with a kiss in my purse, I can't imagine it.

"Good swing, Rollin. You hit that ball a country mile," I say repeating what Dad said whenever I hit a baseball well.

Rollin is four the spring I share my love of baseball with him for the first time. We use the garage door as a backstop and the kitchen cutting board for home plate. I show him how to hold the bat and where to put his feet. I see determination each time he readies himself for a new pitch. With every swing of the bat, Rollin proves he has the talent to play this great American game.

"Grandma, do you think we can play baseball the next time I come over?"

I hug my oldest grandson. "Next time you come over, Rollin, I want you to hit that ball a country mile."

"We're going to Bunnyland," Joshua announces as we head out the front door to walk the dog.

Bunnyland is a strip of grass that separates our subdivision from the neighboring one. Last spring Joshua and I made it to Bunnyland early enough to see bunny families hopping everywhere.

"If we're early we might see Peter Rabbit," I joke with him.

With Joshua, my relationship is different from the other grandchildren. I believe we enjoy each other's company more than anyone else's. When I sweep him up in my arms, he reacts like it's Christmas morning. We collect pinecones and dandelions and, if there's a summer shower, Joshua and I wade through every mud puddle we can find all the way to Bunnyland and back.

Three-year-old Liam sports his kilt with manly pride. He tucks his saffron frock into his clan tartan and hangs a sporran from his belt. On his feet he laces traditional gillie brogues. When he takes a place beside the other Scotsmen in the family, Liam is a man among men.

Just before Liam's birth, I went to see a spiritual medium. She said my daughter's new baby was a boy and would be psychic. For months after Liam was born, our family playfully tossed around remarks about the psychic world. But I scratch my head when I watch grandson Liam from a distance; there's a presence about him that I can't explain.

From his highchair, Morgan sticks his small arm straight out and tucks his head down slightly when I come into the kitchen. "The Force is strong with this one," I say in my best Darth Vader voice.

The Force must be strong because every time Morgan stopped breathing my daughter, Andrea, was able to revive him. There were wild rides to the hospital in the middle of the night. I slept with my clothes on, ready to go on a moment's notice. After the doctors ran tests and found nothing, Andrea and her husband took turns for months holding Morgan until his breathing stabilized.

I reach out and touch fingertips with him before pulling him from the highchair. I whisper in his ear, "The Force is strong with you young Morgan." Then I hold this one a little closer than all the rest.

I expected to marry, buy a house, have children, and join the PTA, but I never expected to be a grandmother. It never entered my thoughts that one day my children would have children of their own. Each time I stand outside the newborn nursery and look through the window at a new grandchild, I know Curly the weather-beaten cowboy with the gravel voice and a cigarette dangling from his lips is right.

The secret of life is one thing, just one thing, and if I stick to that everything else don't mean shit.

WISH LIST

for Goldie

I wish for it to be summer, with the front door open and the screen unlocked. I wish to walk in and see sewing draped over the armchair next to a pincushion in the shape of a red tomato. I wish for an empty coffee cup and the morning papers scattered around the footstool on the living room floor.

"Mom, I'm here."

I wish to stand in the hallway with one foot on the bottom step, my head bent slightly, listening for movement upstairs, while the wall clock ticks and the radio plays country music softly in the kitchen.

"Mom, are you up there?"

I wish to open the basement door and see folding chairs stacked in the landing beside cases of extra pop and bags of groceries headed for the fruit cellar. I wish to see dirty clothes thrown down the stairs to be gathered up one by one in the next trip to the basement laundry.

"Mom, are you down there?"

I wish to walk into the kitchen with the sweet smell of spaghetti sauce bubbling on the stove and breakfast dishes still on the table. I wish to stand beside the china cabinet—overflowing with pictures and mementoes—that took eighty-eight years to collect.

"Mom!"

I wish to open the back door and step into a beautiful garden of roses and clematis with the sprinkler running low.

"Mom, are you out here?"

I wish to look over rows and rows of wooden fencing and see my mother again standing next to her neighbor. I wish for her to be smiling when she waves to me and I wave back. I wish for her to call out, "I'll be right there."

I wish for it to be true.

A CELEBRATION OF THE BUGFLIES

The 4th of July offered more to me last summer than my normal celebration of freedom with fireworks and hotdogs. It was also a celebration of the bugflies.

Our air-conditioning broke just before the holiday weekend. There was no time for repairs, so my husband and I knew we had to make the best of it.

"This will be fun," I told him, as I hung the Betsy Ross flag on the front porch. "The house will be too hot and everyone can enjoy the holiday outside."

We put up a canopy to shade the picnic tables. We bought kiddy pools for the grandchildren, pulled coolers from the basement and filled them with pop and ice. I made salads the night before, while my daughters prepared hot dishes in their air-conditioned apartments.

On the 4th of July temperatures soared to 105 degrees. We ate under the canopy in suffocating heat. If you were a five-year-old sitting in the new wading pool, you were happy. But if you were an adult, you were miserable. By 4:00 everyone had said goodbye. Close to tears, I knew the biggest holiday weekend of the summer had flopped. Only our three-year-old grandson, Joshua, was unaffected by the heat and begged to spend the night.

Nightfall brought no relief from the heat, so we took our leftovers to the backyard. With Joshua between my husband and me, we sat in the glider eating hotdogs and potato salad when the first fireflies appeared.

Like tiny flashbulbs, hundreds lit up the muggy evening with a pulsating radiance. Joshua was captivated by something he had never seen before. With each twinkle he shouted, "Grandma, look there's one. Grandpa, Grandpa, look there's another one." Suddenly this unpleasant day took on new meaning.

Memories came flooding back to me. I ached for a magic formula that would allow me to scoop up my young grandson and sail back over the years towards the laughter of my own grandparents and other summer evenings long ago when foolish kittens jumped for fireflies on a small farm in Murray, Kentucky.

For a few seconds, I was permitted the pleasure of picturing two generations separated by more than fifty years sharing the same space, enjoying together a summer ritual of alluring fireflies as they danced through the backyards of time. I realized, with startled certainty, it was me who bridged the gap, who possessed the magic formula that defied death and allowed those I love to reach across the decades and touch each other briefly.

The glider swayed gently in the still warm twilight. Joshua relaxed into my arms and with a yawn asked, "Grandma can we celebrate the 4th of July with the bugflies next year?"

How lucky our air-conditioning broke just before the holiday weekend.

THE MAN WHOSE CLOTHES DON'T TOUCH HIS BODY

In Berkley's 36th District Court on Valentines Day, eighteen-year-old Raphy Murrell wore a black tuxedo with his long hair pulled back in a ponytail. I expected him to be nervous, but instead he smiled and shook hands with people as they came into the courtroom. *He's definitely a cool cucumber,* I thought from my front row seat. Raphy was not here for a court date involving a criminal offense; he was waiting to marry my youngest daughter.

I met Raphy one month earlier coming out of my daughter Andrea's bedroom at 6:00 in the morning.

"Who are you," I asked this skinny stranger while grabbing frantically at my bathrobe, "and why are you in my house?"

"It's not a problem," he said on his way out the front door.

"Andrea," I shouted up the stairs, "who was that boy and why was he in your bedroom?" My voice increased in volume the more this situation sank in.

"There's nothing to be concerned about," she shouted back. "We're getting married next month."

Thinking this was a joke, my response was simple, "You can't marry him; he's too skinny. His clothes don't touch his body."

My oldest daughter, Lisa, came out of her first floor bedroom. "Mom," she whispered, "Andrea's getting married on Valentine's Day at Berkley City Hall. She already has her dress."

"This is insane; she's still in high school," I said. "Andrea, you're not living here if you get married," I screamed up the stairs pushing pregnancy from my mind.

Andrea got out of bed and appeared at the top of the stairs wearing a Guns n' Roses t-shirt. "Mom," she said calmly, "I'm not pregnant. I'm eighteen years old, and there's nothing you can do about it. Besides, we're going to live at Raphy's house. His mother said we could live there if he cleans his bedroom."

I had gone to bed living on Tyler Street and woken up in a nut barn. I turned around and walked into the bathroom, "I'm going to work," I shouted over my shoulder, "where it's easier to anticipate chaos."

I had one month to learn about Raphy, my son-in-law-to-be. His real name is Robert, but for some reason people called him Raphy. He dropped out of high school and works at a Valvoline station doing oil changes on cars. He drove his parents' minivan because his car didn't run. When he came to our house for dinner a few weeks before the wedding, I asked him to remove his oily work boots. Instead, he lay on the front porch and stared at the sky while he smoked cigarettes. I asked if I could bring his food outside, but he replied, "It's not a problem."

Raphy must have cleaned his room because Andrea moved all her things to his house the day before the wedding.

"Are you going to finish high school?" I asked while she packed.

"Of course I'm finishing high school," she answered. "With only three months left, why wouldn't I?"

"Would you like me to pick you up for school?" Thinking of all the mornings I had to entice her out of bed by promising McDonald's breakfast. "I could stop for you on my way to work," I offered.

"No," she said nonchalantly. "Raphy's mom said she would take me."

Raphy's best man showed up at the wedding wearing a leather jacket, blue jeans and the greasiest hair I've ever seen. Apparently that wasn't a problem either. The two of them stood beside the Mayor of Berkley waiting for Andrea and her bridesmaid to walk from the holding pen where criminals are kept, past the wedding guests to the front of the courtroom. I turned to my husband, who had come home from work the last five days, gone straight to bed and said, "I give this marriage six months, a year if one of them learns to cook."

After the reception at a Chinese restaurant, Raphy and Andrea sat at the dining room table and opened wedding cards. His parents' van was parked in the driveway to be used for their honeymoon in Chicago. I caught a glimpse of the future watching how well Raphy worked with my daughter. They talked quietly discussing expenses for the trip and money to be put aside to fix his car. It seemed nothing was a problem for Raphy Murrell.

I gave them a map of Michigan and a travel book on Chicago. When they left, Raphy drove the van too fast down Tyler Street. I waved good-bye and wondered if I would see my daughter and the man whose clothes don't touch his body alive again. Then I leaned against the front door and slid slowly to the floor.

THE GLASS PARTITION

While my daughter, Lisa, browses for a party dress in an up-scale dress shop, six-year-old granddaughter, Elizabeth, and I look through the glass partition at a young woman in a wedding dress.

"Isn't she lovely?" I whisper to Elizabeth as the woman moves slowly around on the pedestal in front of a wall of mirrors. The strapless gown has a beautiful sequined bodice that melts into yards and yards of shimmering silky-smooth satin flowing elegantly to the floor.

"Someday you may wear a dress like that," I tell my granddaughter with chocolate cookie smears on her face.

Pressing our noses against the glass like peeping Toms, we see hundreds of gowns crowding every inch of this area divided off from the rest of the store by glass partitions. Racks of gowns line the walls; freestanding racks stand in rows, all styles and sizes, allowing only enough room to walk single file through this creamy white forest.

Elizabeth looks up, "Grandma can we go inside and see the bride?" she asks.

It dawns on me once again I'm on the outside looking in at this mysterious cultural phenomenon I don't understand called The Great American Wedding.

As a hippie chick, my marriage vows were said in sandals and a flowered dress that I had worn to a rock concert the weekend before. The most expensive thing at my wedding was the marijuana we took with us on our honeymoon. Thank goodness my daughters' lives never warranted big weddings. It is inconceivable to me that the price tag on these lavish one-day affairs could equal a down payment on a new home. The endless flow of money it took to raise children kept my husband and me juggling our finances for years.

"Grandma, I want to go in and see the bride," Elizabeth insists.

The young woman finishes her alterations, steps down from the pedestal and disappears into a backroom just as Elizabeth blasts on the scene. With her chunky little-girl body, hair hanging, pant legs too short showing too much sock and sandal, she mounts the pedestal like a queen.

In front of the wall of mirrors I watch my gawky granddaughter lift her arms gracefully and twirl around and around until she transforms herself into a beautiful bride. Wanting to be part of her fantasy, I feel myself pulled into this strange world of gowns and veils, until I see Elizabeth, many years from now and quite grown up, turning to me and asking, "Grandma isn't my wedding dress lovely?" With Elizabeth's lust for living there is no way she could ever pass up this expensive slice of life. Elizabeth will want a huge wedding.

I see Lisa coming toward us through the glass partition.

"Mom, you might get in trouble being in here," she says. "What are you two doing?"

I look at my daughter and say with a smile, "We're spending your retirement money."

THE FINE ART OF FIDDLIN'
in memory of Big John, who always gave more than he took

Oh, how I love to fiddle. To move about from one task to another, not really accomplishing anything, just fiddlin'. To fiddle away the weekend is a luxury beyond belief. I have to wear old clothes because fiddlin' could take me anywhere. I might end up deep in the mud pulling weeds from the garden or maybe down in the creek bed searching for stones to landscape the yard. Sometimes fiddlin' can be two-fold. While organizing the storage area under the basement stairs, I find my old baseball glove and realize it must be oiled immediately. I've never understood why people need expensive vacations to relax; all they have to do is learn to fiddle.

I've watched Dad fiddle an afternoon away cleaning out his fishing tackle box. His hair combed straight back always created a ragged crest at the back of his head and earned him the nickname, "Kingfisher." He would set himself up in the backyard under a tree. "I'm holding down the shade," he would say perched on a wooden chair, his large head and short body contributing to the illusion of a Belt Kingfisher waiting to dive headfirst into water. With his cigarettes and lighter close at hand, Dad told stories about fishing the Mississippi River bottom as a young boy and, by the time the tackle box was wiped clean and all the bobbers and flies were returned to their rightful place, I had a clearer understanding of this man forty-six years my senior.

Mom's untidy house proved beyond a doubt she was queen of the fiddlers. It was a cozy place, this fiddle house, because no matter where you sat there were interesting fiddle piles to explore. Mom dropped her fiddles along the way, like Hansel and Gretel, hoping to find her way back to them someday. I've seen her multi-fiddle, working her way from the messy basement sewing room, through the kitchen to stir the dinner pot, and end up in the yard planting a rose bush. Mom was a wonder at fiddlin' the day she left bags and bags of unpacked groceries sitting in a hot kitchen while she read the story, *"Hey, Diddle Diddle, The Cat and the Fiddle"* to her granddaughter.

My sister, Connie, married a fiddler, but she is not one. Brother-in-law, John, has fine-tuned fiddlin' with age. I'm envious of his experienced fiddlin'. His garage is a palace for fiddlin'. If you need a certain size nut or bolt, or maybe an old push mower, he will fiddle around inside until he finds it. With the passing of my parents, it's up to John and me to keep fiddlin' alive in the family.

This spring when I cleaned out the flowerbeds with my granddaughter, Elizabeth, I realized we have a new fiddler in the family. She's only six but can fiddle with the best of us. While we raked, Elizabeth and I sang the crawdad song and played with the neighborhood cats. It was a wonderful afternoon of family fiddlin'.

From the front porch Mike called to us in the yard, "What are you two doing? I thought you were raking."

"We're fiddlin'," I answered. My husband doesn't understand fiddlin'. He's not a fiddler.

LUCKY LOTTO DAY

Husband Mike is pouting. He didn't win the lottery this week. He takes the loss personally on Sunday mornings before church when he checks the lotto numbers from the night before, hoping the winning ones are his.

"Well, we didn't win jack-shit," Mike loves to say. "But the good news is, neither did anyone else." He hates the thought of giving his retirement money to strangers. Mike's convinced Michigan's Mega Lotto Jackpot will solve all our problems, will be the answer to our prayers.

I admit it would be nice to set up trust funds for each of the five grandchildren. Pay off the mortgage on our home. Perhaps help our daughters with a business venture or maybe take a first class vacation with the entire family. It's fun to dream of endless riches—piles and piles of free money—but I worry instant wealth could cause too many ripples in our humdrum family puddle.

As Mike lies back in his recliner practicing what he will say to his boss when lucky lotto day arrives, I picture our grandchildren sitting on the front porch talking to the local news. I can already hear eight-year-old grandson, Rollin, with his fascination for bodily functions, telling family tales.

"My grandmother farted yesterday when she lifted my baby brother into his car seat," Rollin would happily share with the world. With TV cameras rolling, Rollin and his six-year-old brother, Joshua, would demonstrate how it happened, accompanied by fart noises in two-part harmony along with a chorus of giggles and hysterical laughter. Embarrassing family secrets would burst forth from the mouths of babes to the delight of every newspaper reporter in the city.

Mike's love of fast cars could finally become a reality if we had millions in the bank.

"We'll need to go to Italy," he would announce one evening after dinner. "They interview you personally when you buy a Ferrari. Each Ferrari is custom-built to fit the buyer. They'll take my measurements."

"Probably a good thing," I say looking at his ballooning waistline.

"What's the cost of this blessed event?" I ask.

"Less than you think, only a mil, maybe a mil and a half."

"Is this the kind of car I can take to the grocery store?" the practical side of me will need to know.

It would be difficult maintaining a sense of normalcy with so much money just waiting to be spent. A life-long dream of an eighteen-foot Day

Sailor, pulled behind the family car and launched at Stony Creek Metro Park, would suddenly become an 80-foot ocean cruiser that sleeps twenty.

"What would you think about sailing around the world with a few friends next week?" Mike would ask looking up from the financial page.

"What about pirates?"

"You worry too much," he would answer frowning.

"My retirement dream of a one-room log cabin on a few quiet acres in the middle of a Michigan pine forest would be traded for a log mansion with an indoor basketball court somewhere on the Continental Divide. There would be no stopping this tidal wave of Lucky Lotto spending that would hit our family with the force of a tsunami. As we fought to keep from drowning, treacherous waters would separate us from all things sensible.

"Do you want the good news or the bad news?" Mike wants to know on Sunday morning after checking his lotto numbers.

"Only good news," I reply to the left-brained love of my life.

"No one else won, either," he informs me.

"Do you remember what *The Rolling Stones* said forty years ago, Mike?"

"I can't get no satisfaction?"

"You don't always get what you want, but you get what you need," I quote the ancient rock group that—to my surprise—can still sing and dance at the same time on stage.

On the way to church in our Ford Focus that fits us perfectly, I'm comfortable with the odds that Lucky Lotto Day will probably never find its way to our humdrum family puddle. If all it takes is Michigan's Mega Lotto Jackpot to solve our problems, we really don't have any.

THE GREEN FELT HAT

Hake Hassan enters the funeral home for the Mass of a five-year-old boy. Having witnessed life from both sides of the Atlantic Ocean during two world wars, this elderly Albanian woman is no stranger to death. As a young woman her small frame supported ten pregnancies, but now it is a web of brittle bones under tired skin seasoned from decades of sun and hard work. Her once thick black hair has turned white, and she wears it pulled back in a bun. A few strands have come loose and curl, like lace, around the edges of a green felt hat that sits squarely on top of her head. At eighty-six, Hake Hassan still projects an air of feistiness, a trait she learned upon arriving at Ellis Island from Albania many years ago.

She handles sadness with poise when she speaks with the grieving family about the accidental drowning. Throughout the dimly lit room she hears muffled sobs. Most in the room struggle for the right words. It is a relief when the Mass begins.

She picks a chair nearest the fish tank, removes her hat and sits it on top of the tank. To her surprise, she watches in disbelief as the hat appears inside the glass aquarium—swinging to and fro—the fuzzy vessel looks at home in this underwater world moving gracefully among the fish while air bubbles escape from under its brim and race to the surface. When it finally reaches bottom the green felt hat settles squarely on top of a sunken pirate ship.

The tension subsides in the room as smiles appear here and there. With all eyes on this Albanian immigrant who has mastered a second language, and taught herself to drive a Model T, she rises from her chair with the same spirit that had propelled her through Ellis Island and into a new world. For more then sixty years, Hake Hassan has known the procedure for dealing with the unexpected. She begins by rolling up her sleeves.

WAITING FOR THE DEER

I read the other students' essays after arriving home tonight from the writing workshop. I finish, turn the lights out and sit at the window. I'm waiting for the deer. They travel through my hosta garden, tiptoeing while I sleep, across the back of the property, ducking tree branches, leaving their pointed prints and nibbles off this flower or that for me to find in the morning. In the face of self-doubt, I'm looking for comfort in the dark.

The British novelist, Evelyn Waugh, once said, "I put the words down and push them a bit." This business of writing is a bit harder than I thought. Tonight, as my eyes strain for signs of deer, I can't understand why I would wish this constant word pushing upon myself. Even in dreams I'm pushing words.

I lean forward and look west toward the creek. The deer will cross under Walton Boulevard through a large culvert, then jump from the creek bed one by one and follow each other just inside the tree line to my garden paradise. I'm reminded of a story I read about the caribou in the Arctic National Wildlife Refuge and how they have migrated on the same trails across the arctic tundra for 20,000 years. The environmentalists call this the last wild place. A Native American says when he looks out over Brown Bear River and Snowy Owl Mountain, "The trails come alive each spring when the caribou come to breed. Everything has a name here and everything has a story."

The stories at the workshop tonight were more than I expected. They leaped off the page at me. "Pounding memories" is how one writer remembered his emotional journey to the United States from Czechoslovakia. "Going mobile with flame" is how another described leaving church as a child on Christmas Eve with a lit candle. One writer wrote how jogging brought her "a sense of freedom, a tempo, a power."

A rustle from the pines turns my head. A ragtag deer herd breaks the tree line and parades wild beauty into my moonlit garden. Self-doubt fades and I immediately start pushing words, searching for the right ones to describe the comfort and reassurance I've found in my own last wild place.

The kitchen light silhouettes my husband. "Why are you sitting in the dark?" he whispers.

"I'm waiting for the deer."

REFLECTIONS FROM THE GRIEVING POOL

Mary Ellen Soroka

My journey with writing begins in a place I call *the grieving pool.* I wade into the waters. I submerge my sorrow for five years after my mother's passing. A hysterectomy engages me to drift through ideas while my words well up into poetry. My mind washes away from a head injury and grief over Dad's death, and I sink into being alone. I resurface, immersed in words, now treading ripples of ink that glide from my pen. I swim through writing with a joyful spirit for creating short stories and poems. Writing my way through grief saves me from drowning, and in my pool of suffering my humanity swells. I know there are people who also swim in that pool. If my writing connects with them and helps them grieve a loss of any kind, I have my audience.

I find words for free-verse poems from many different resources. Scripture inspires the poem, *Easy Spirit.* "You were knit together in your mother's womb" (Psalm 139:13) becomes "I was stitched together by the hands." I watch myself on a family film that captures my eleventh birthday and record my feelings of the moment with the poem, *Hiding in Full View.* I have a relationship with a window in my home. Every day I sit on my sofa and listen and watch. One day rain mixes with the question "What do you want?"and becomes the poem *Dissolving.*

By my bedside I stash pens and a journal. I keep a journal on my kitchen counter, in the glove compartment of my car and in my pocket while walking because I don't know how or when my inner poet will awaken. In my routine of walking around Lake Sixteen, the sight of autumn leaves swirling beneath my feet stirs my memory of the colors in the first dress Mom made me. "Leaves of russet, burnt umber and ocher" becomes the first line of the short story *Mom Makes Pretty.*

Try this:

Keep a small journal by your bedside and write your dreams before you get out of bed in the morning. Be careful not to analyze, just copy what you saw and what you felt during the dream. Let images tell the story and let them reveal their meaning without conjecture. Don't worry if your dream seems bizarre or strange, just keep writing. Sometimes your muse will be inspired and you'll be able to begin a poem from what you've written, and sometimes you'll want to set notes aside and look back through your recorded dreams later that month. My dreams created my poems *In My Dream State* and *Consider.*

IN MY DREAM STATE

Up small hills of painted color,
along the meadows of quiet,
near uprooted pines is a man
in a camel coat.
Where am I going? I wonder.
There are no directions for where you're going.

I look past his left shoulder to
a hickory tree with its center carved out.
Metal hands of a clock:
big hand on twelve,
small hand on eleven.
From the tree buds, letters float.
T i m e   h a s   s t o p p e d.

Scathed birches surround me,
leaves within the wind;
their points of stars
tip over themselves.

In a waif woods I slip into a blue pond.
My hands cling to slender water reeds.
Dear God, why am I in this grieving pool?
Through the lilies of the valley my tears fall
and I pour out my soul.

I'm snow light, swell whole
into another place.
I'm home—
not one I've known.

DISSOLVING

Tapping the window
light rain in small quantities
flows into longer streams.

I concentrate the touch
of my fingertips
against emerging wetness,
each occurrence random
in a room rich with abstinence.

My face flush
on his bare rug of a chest,
his heart rhythm echoes
inside its walls
a soft pillowy sound.

His question between us:
What do you want?
My unrevealed response.

Syllables are patterned after the rainfall.
My words are sprinkled with inconsistencies
inhibited by a generous amnesia.

I only remember the rain.

MY SLOW CHANGES

Before my car accident, all I want is change; afterward, my mind becomes a concentration camp. One hard strike to my left temple; I'm in a dimension with every word dissected and my excessive thoughts diminished to focus in the moment. I say to my husband, "Chuck, I need one of those." My eyes narrow, as if I've typed letters across a screen. *D I S H* appears in my mind. The word is? *D I S H.* The word is? My forehead furrows, *D I S H.*

"Bring me the round thing we put food on," I say.

"I'm leaving for work now. Are you all right?" Chuck, asks.

"I'm okay." Intense sensory stimulations to my neurons appear as flashes of tiny lights coming in too fast. "I'm going grocery shopping. Let's see, my keys are?"

The grocery store has all those aisles of choices: cereals, soups, soaps and too many kinds of bread. Too much information. I won't go today. I walk over to the dining room table. I take my pen and open the journal. At the top of the page I write, *union,* beneath this, *together, join, assimilate, match pair, apple, core, deep, push.* At the top of the page I write, *separate.* Beneath this I write, *apart, beyond, space, time, travel, distance, speed, lightness, darkness.* Ring, ring, ring. Ignore the phone. I stare at the words; my pen moves. Eyes to the words. My pen moves. My mind shifts as I write:

Synthesis

Distance pushes a matched pair, beyond the center of comfort,
like the union between the apple skin and core
is measured through a white darkness,
beyond the space which joins them.
They assimilate through being apart,
traveling deep into the lightness of separation.

Layer of dust on my wild cherry hutch. I wonder if Laurie will recover. Not enough dust to wipe off but enough to write on. Maybe I should call her. Let's see, what was I going to do? I don't remember. My shoulders slump, my eyes close and my head tilts.

"Roll, roll, roll, go with the flow," a friend said.

"My car keys are with the strap in the thing I carry on my shoulder," I say. I'll feel better walking along Lake Sixteen with the rhythm of my own nature. The flow takes me to water. I step on stones on the shore of Lake Sixteen.

I walk back, turn the ignition on, and warm air fills the car. I finger the page of my journal. I have no urgent sense to fill the space soon or quickly spoil the space I'm in. Sunsets calm me. Sunlight on the horizon spreads like apple butter, outlines trees' black bark, sinks into ice-white water.

In my black journal, I write: *Water creases caress honey grass, bobbing chickadee lilies. A slate sky with steel clouds in a Wrigley wrapper red horizon. Bark wood hammock shelters a piney squirrel. A cinnamon tree glistens with leafy air.*

"You can be a site-specific introvert," my mentor Marlys said.

Home again, I decide to go to bed. Blanket on, blanket off. I turn to my right, then to my left. The back of my head, jab, pin, pain. I rub the throbbing place. Yellow light cracks through the shade. When I'm exposed to a stressful circumstance, the door into my consciousness closes with a steel slam. *Oh, Lord, why does my head hurt so much?* I cradle the phone.

"Reverend Christine, is that you?"

"Yes."

"I was wondering if I could talk with you about my head injury. Why can't I sleep?"

"What did you do yesterday?"

"I talked for three hours on the phone."

"Oh, they're talking into your ear, directly into your head." Six inches away I see the round small holes of the phone and hear her voice continue.

"There's no body, no space, to separate your neurons from being over-stimulated."

"I try to recall details—so draining."

"Give yourself the idea of whom or what to let in your head. Give yourself space."

"Thank you, Reverend, for your help. Goodbye."

"Space, create space, in my life, how do I create more space?" I say. Chuck's blue eyes look into mine.

"It's like a brick in the wall. Take the brick out; there's a space and the wall doesn't fall. See what fills the space," he replies.

Norway maple leaves, rosebush, heart-shaped foliage. Sun warms my face. I sit on a green lawn chair. A dragonfly clings onto a faded brown stem. Its core, crimson red and webbed wings, centers its movement.

You can fly in stillness, I whisper to its wings.

VISION

I see her in the flesh,
a ghost of my past,
slowly stepping towards her duty.

Her female gravity
thin in baggy jeans.

She is heavy with thoughts
of obligations and commitments
she shall keep.

A pale apparition
closer to the past than ever before
she carries a sigh for compensation.

I want to approach her
to speak my voice unmoved.

VEILED

Dad drives Mom, John and me across the Center Street Bridge. I watch cobalt smoke come out of the long pipe of the steel mill. It drapes the light blue sky like a veil. It covers all who live in the Mahoning Valley with a vile touch on the skin, in the lungs, especially my grandfather, father and his brothers who labor there.

My father wears the mill on his skin, sometimes heavily like a wool blanket of coal. He washes it off in the shower stall he built in the basement, a daily routine depending on which shift he drew. He stands under the showerhead of clear clean water, rubs the dark pigment layered on his skin that only lye can scrub off; it leaves sprinkled graphite specks on the white tile like steel slivers. There are months he is clean because of the temporary layoffs by the bosses at Republic Steel. He saves a portion of his paycheck from the overtime to help us over the lean weeks ahead.

He disdains his work; with no high school diploma, he's trapped in the tracks, creating hopeless quiet places I can't reach. His distance becomes like the sound of the train whistle I hear from the mill. A long, lonely, sound—far and unreachable—it travels over the hamlets of Youngstown, from Briar Hill to Monkey's Nest and Lansingville, up from the valley, reaching through the window of the bedroom I share with John. Those whistle sounds from the mill's railroad yard pull back and away from us, take the brakeman, our dad, with them. He's on the short end of the tracks, and steam from the engine pulls him up and down the line with no destination.

Dad has no control over his employment within that solid place of steel and coal, but his talent for telling stories creates riveting laughter. When he can't tell stories, Dad's emotions burst like a blast furnace, with short, hot, fiery combustion from his lungs.

A smoky haze layers my emotions the way my bridal veil touches the edge of my eyelashes. I walk down the aisle of Saint Dominic's Church. I blink through its soft irritations. Dad lifts the creamy netting. I'm marrying away from his bursts, yet I carry the fury into my marriage, a layer in my lungs not quite clear of the smoky gray.

DAD'S WIRELESS CONNECTION

Endocarditis—the doctors diagnose a blood disease Dad contracted a year ago.

"He'll need antibiotics every four hours for eight weeks," the doctor states.

"One of us needs to take care of him," my brother John replies. "Can't you take care of my dad?"

"I can't do that, John." Ironically, I'm severely anemic and will need an operation to remove fibroid tumors from my uterus. Imagine a social worker who's worked in gerontology not able to take care of her own father. Yet, I understand my brother's response.

"I can bring Dad to Michigan and get him in a place," I say. "I'm sick. I'll need an operation in three months." The words spill out in the air like a bubble bursting over his head. The letters separate, spill down and scatter onto the floor, lie flat, unheard. His eyes widen and his shoulders pull back.

"I'll do it, I'll take care of my dad," he says.

Dad starts the new year and endures eight weeks of medicine. Like a runner in training, his body pumps the liquid antibiotics through their course, and they sweat out of his body. He survives, but there's damage to his heart valve. Dad has an operation to repair it the same week I have my surgery. A few months later, a golf buddy of Dad's phones John.

"There's something wrong with your Dad when he's on the golf course." He's missing pieces, like in a puzzle jumbled out of the box. His brain is challenged to move them around. With each stroke, he attempts to fill the spaces, to assemble a whole picture. He lost a big piece after his wife died.

"Mary Ellen, I'm bringing Dad here to live with me."

A few months later: "I have to sell his house and we need to pack up his belongings the weekend of October 28th," John says. So many possessions in a lifetime, we decide which treasures are attached to a memory and which collect dust. My ears are wired into headphones playing music. Between layers of Mom's tea towels, I nest each plate, cup, and saucer of her Christmas china. Dad purchased them in Japan when he was stationed in Korea.

"Can I have this milk glass bowl?" Carol, the housekeeper, asks.

"Yes," I sigh, "I guess, I can't take it all." But I wish I had more time to sort through accumulated artifacts with a memory glued on, like the glass jar I made in Blue Birds, with decorated emerald stones rimmed with a black-gold design. Mom's kept treasure. My home has no extra room for all my childhood treasures. I carry away books, with memories of Mom's voice reading to me and John: *Little Black Sambo, A Child's Garden of Verse* and *Shirley Temple's Storybook*. Dad built this house, now it is out of his hands. My brother comes up the basement steps.

"Bell wire!" John says.

"What?" I respond.

"Bell wire!" Chuck says.

"What do you mean, *bell wire?*" I say.

"As in telephone wire," Chuck answers.

"Dad wired the basement with it. All those lights, it will never pass code," John says.

"You've got that right, you know Dad. If he could find a way to do it on the cheap, he would," I state.

"We'll have an electrician re-wire the basement."

Leaves turn amber, crimson, ocher and gold. We gather apples and pumpkins from the earth. We assemble around a Thanksgiving harvest at cousin Debbie's home.

"Uncle John, do your invisible flea trick," Deb requests of my dad.

"Get him a paper bag, Mom," cousin Brian says. Dad's long fingers fold over the top of the brown paper bag.

"Where's that invisible flea?" His eyes dart around.

"Oh, there it is." With his left index finger and thumb, he pinches the air.

"Got it! Now I will throw the flea and catch it in the bag." His arm moves downward and up, his thumb and finger release the flea. The paper moves up and down, and my second cousins and my nieces hear a snap of sound. They laugh and, like a firecracker on the Fourth of July, Dad lights up with a sudden sparkle that's quickly gone.

Months later, Dad can't find the memory attached to the emotion or person. The wires in his brain are disconnected by a mini-stroke, and a switch flips OFF.

"Dad had another stroke," John says. I can't connect an emotion to what I hear, my brain injured in a car accident. Like the aftermath of an earthquake in my brain, there's a vast stillness in my memory. Dad and I are in the same place, a million brain cells can't connect to communicate. His skill to tell a funny story is gone, and the invisible flea will remain in the air.

Autumn falls with Thanksgiving at Debbie's home again, and the air in their house is mixed with my adolescent feelings of tension. The wire in my brain that connects my words could snap at any moment. I'm like a walker on a tightwire with my words, but I continue speaking. I read my poem, *Hiding In Full View*, to my cousin, Chrissy:

Focus on the freeze-framed appearances
captured in the canister of film.
Look at the edited emotions,
of an undeveloped girl.

Roll back the black and white negatives.
Staged reactions shifting her off center,
play in production to the eye of the camera.

View the scenes of how the image splits
the continuity of her development.
See this image of an interrupted girl
fade to black.

Advance to this moment;
she writes what she will not say.
Poems process the essence of her emotions,
developing the girl.

Watch how she projects her scripted image,
feed fresh film into the projector,
photograph a focused soul.

"Dad, do you remember saying to me there are only two kinds of people in the world, Ukrainians and people who want to be Ukrainians?"
"Yesss."A silent energy flows between us like within the bell wire.

Months later, I sit in my stairwell. Through the window, leaves of the oak trees wave on a breeze, compelling me to drive to Lake Sixteen. Trees cantilever over the path to shelter me. *I love you, Daddy,* I say into the air. Words climb the pine tree, fly into the sky, carried by the wire of the wind to Ohio. *I know you can hear me.* At five o'clock, my feet are still. *If you can make it until Thursday, I will come, your delicate body like a bird. You return to your name, Soroka, which means magpie in Ukrainian.*
    I enter my kitchen. An illuminated halo light on my phone blinks.
    "You have one new message, March fifth. Message received at five-twenty."
    "Mary Ellen, it's your brother, John. Dad died at five today."
    Simulated female voice continues, "You have no more new messages."

GOLFING WITH GOD

Dad on dawn patrol,
from his gravesite to the 9th hole
across the street.

What's it like on God's golf course?
Are there natural fairways, without roughs?
Maybe God spots you a mulligan, off the tee,
for all the fun you gave to people.

I guess you have no need for those
Lacosta shirts we bought you.
Who gets the honor when you tee off?

In paradise your ball hits the sweet spot.
Never a bogey, always under par,
a birdie or eagle on the long drive.

There are no handicaps in heaven.

MOM MAKES PRETTY

The first dress I remember that Mom makes for me has leaves of russet, burnt umber and ochre, with three-quarter length sleeves and a white peter pan collar. I'm just old enough to walk. The last dress she makes me has a high bodice and a scooped neckline, puffy short sleeves and circles of mauve flowers on beige cotton; its length falls to my knees.

My cousin, Debbie, announces a June wedding. My dress is mint green to the floor with shoes and straw hat to match the bridal party. Mom's hands are free. Vogue's white envelope is between her fingers, and the light brown faded tissue slides out. Crinkle, crinkle, and the folds unfold until the translucency of the tissue becomes transparent with dark brown lines and unconnected dots. She will transfer some to the fabric with blue tailor's chalk. Her fingers move along the black crêpe and the tissue. A quarter-inch from the cutting line, at right angles, she presses straight silver pins, like stick women, into the fabric.

"These are the good scissors," she says, holding them like a trophy, "only for cutting material." One blade of the shears rests on the table. The other moves down toward the fabric in long slashes like a kid taking giant steps. It slows at the curves of the brown lines where her hips will move and the seams come together. She pulls the solid pine top up and to the left; it lays flat. Her left hand is on the black metal, and she pulls the machine out. In silver lettering it says, *Singer*. The black spool slides down on the one-inch metal top. Between Mom's thumb and finger, thread moves to the left, loops through the eyehole at the top, runs down the curved round wire through and back into the tiny oblong hole of the needle. Her hands look as if she is conducting a symphony. *Ta Da, Ta Da, Ta Da, Da Da. Ta Da, Ta Da, Ta Da, Da Da.*

Her fingers are on the ear of the machine as it moves slowly forward and backward. On the base between two pieces of silver through a thin, dark space, the thread hooks in and it's connected to the machine. *Ta Da!*

Black material slides under the thick, two-pronged fork; with one movement of her thumb and wrist she seals the fabric tight; her fingers are flat on each side of the fabric. She presses on a raised button of the metal black box on the floor. She's careful to avoid the straight pins as the needle jumps up and down through fabric. With elbows out, she conducts a final crescendo, and pieces are needled together through fabric as it inches down the back of the pine cabinet. A cascade of crêpe. She refines the shape of the triangle on the front, which will open up for her cleavage to show.

"This dress will have an invisible zipper for the seamless look." She gives a gentle press with a steam iron, not to damage the crêpe, hems up the dress five-eighths of an inch, at knee length. With her model shoulders and elegant way, my mother descends a staircase. Her blond hair styled, my mother, Margaret, steps out in her Vogue designer black dress.

I'm proud to say Mom made my clothes. Even though I attended sewing classes in sixth grade and high school, I didn't enjoy sewing, but I did inherit her shoulders and that grace to descend a staircase. This Mother's Day it will be twelve years since Mom passed, and writing this make me feel like I've spent time with her.

YOU COULD NOT GO ALONE

I feel out of myself. Mom has come out of surgery with the cancer in her breast contained. One week later, my husband, Chuck, and I travel four hours from Michigan to Ohio. I run under a clear blue sky to my parents' front door to protect the flowers from the cold. The sun's brightness bounces off the snow. The cold is deceiving from the inside of a warm home. I enter the kitchen and place flowers on the sea green counter. She walks quite well considering her multiple sclerosis.

"Oh, flowers, they're beautiful. Mary Ellen, could you help me with something?" Mom says with a smile.

"Yes,"

"I walk like an elephant," she says. "I shake my head from side to side." *She's too thin for an elephant.* She steps on the balls of her feet, pauses and teeters back to the heel in her walk down the hall. Up the stairs, her right hand is red tight on the handrail. She walks along the hall with her fingers pinching the chair railing. I am one step behind her. Her hand on the bedspread, she turns and sits. Her fingers grab the buttons of her blouse. A thin tube hangs from the skin of her breast.

"Could you help me aspirate the fluid? Your father might not be able to do this."

"Yes, Dad isn't much on doctoring." I adjust the tube and she aspirates the fluid.

Her doctors report that her tests are negative. With comfort tucked inside our hearts along with hope for her recovery, we return to Michigan. I call her a week later on a Friday evening. She sounds wistful.

"I don't feel right," she says.

"Call your doctor," I suggest. I hesitate to call her Saturday; one day won't make a difference. I'll wait until Sunday.

Sunday morning Mom wakes. Her feet creep forward while her hands grip the walls. Her fibrillating heart flutters like wings of a butterfly. Her legs give and her cheek crushes on the wear-like-iron carpet. Her cat-green eyes glance upward to Dad. Her heartbeat slows, her veins close, and blood rushes from her heart.

"John I can't breathe; call an ambulance." His features dissolve from her eyes; the warmth fades from her face. The soul floats through blessed prayers of forgiveness. An aura of love remains. My father calls and says,

"Your mother fell to the floor."

"Call an ambulance."

"I did. They're here; I have to go."

I pull drawers out with lingerie, sweaters, wool socks, and then wait, just wait, half an hour to call the hospital, my hand on thick stockings. I step onto the tile, open the cabinet, grab the deodorant, wait, little bottle of shampoo, small toothpaste, mousse gel, tampons just in case, wait. My feet are on the rough carpet of the hall. I'm walking into the spare bedroom to the closet. My fingers wrap around the cold black handle of the luggage. I sit on the bed with the receiver in my hand. I press the buttons slowly.

"Emergency Room South Side Hospital," a nurse answers.

"Margaret Soroka was brought into emergency. Could you tell me her status?"

"I don't know what happened at the house, but when your mother arrived here she had no vitals."

The black receiver of the cordless phone is the connection that joins me to my brother, John. His wife, Becky, answers.

"Mom died," I say.

"John, your mom died," she softy repeats.

I walk to the closet, as his howl echoes in my memory, and remove the black, two-piece, knit sweater-suit Mom and I bought four years earlier for my mother-in-law's funeral. I remember Mom gripping the chair railing on the wall, and saying, "I want to die in my home, and I want to die quickly."

Turnpike, fast food, a sandwich between my fingers with my teeth imprints—I remove the soft bun. Within the crust are thin chicken layers. I don't think this is real chicken; it doesn't look like chicken, and it doesn't taste like it. I decide to stop eating fast food.

I walk into my parents' home and my cousin, a nurse, is with my father, who sits at the dinette table. Dad's lower lip moves up and down. He speaks, soundlessly. His big cow eyes look through me.

"I cried most of the way here," I say, gazing into John's gray-blue eyes.

Rubbing my hands together, I shiver. A bathroom to my right, the chapel's to my left, doors to the sanctuary open. In front of me, I see candle boxes, the vestibule of Saint Charles church. I haven't been here for years.

Well, Mom, you got what you wanted, but I never got a chance to say goodbye.

The funeral director's hands wave toward the light mahogany casket. I don't move. I'm in mannequin motion. Chuck touches my elbow, and that moves my arm forward along with my legs. Posed, with a made-up face, next to the coffin, I slant my feet downward on the carpet of the aisle. Posed, with my non-reflective hazel eyes, I look yet don't see because the haze in my head moves me. *Mom, you are here with us but not with us.* At the pew, Chuck and I slide in along with Dad, John, Becky, and their two daughters. *Where's Mom?*

Her close friend, Paul, gives the eulogy. They had a friendship in spiritual pursuits at church. With the podium positioned before him, he gives an oration. He's a public speaker who has his own radio show. My daze clears for a moment.

"I came here today to say *Auf wiedersehen* to my dear friend, Margaret," Paul says.

Paul descends from the elevated floor to the aisle. He enters his pew, lowers himself on the oak bench. He inhales rapidly, stutters and pauses, inhales between breaths, as if a string were wrapped around God's finger. A gentle movement by God pulls him. Lifts his weight. His shoulders shift down; his head lowers, as if he has nodded to sleep. Like a child who has stayed awake too long, he releases into a limp, Charlie Chaplin slump and falls silently onto the bench of the pew. Everything seems surreal. My mind reaches out to lighten his fall into grace. Loud whispers in the church sound like a prayer, *Our Father.*

My mother's godchild and a cousin perform cardio-pulmonary resuscitation.

We're ushered into a hollow vestibule. The emergency medical technicians arrive. In the silence, Paul crosses the threshold into eternal life.

You couldn't go alone, Mom. You took a friend.

LIFE BREATHS

Mary Ellen, a toddler in an oxygen tent with pneumonia

Little baby breaths, little baby breaths—
breathe little girl. Remember to fill your lungs
with sweet air while you float in your world
under a milk-washed bubble.

Breathe little girl, you could be slowly dying,
your world turned upside-down
with fever and delirium.

Delirium leads to delusion,
a breath away from loss.
Can you go forward and live as the whirl
of your words leaves others behind?

Air fills your eyes, water pours,
sight is swollen—
air infuses your lungs by such winds,
if you were smaller, you would blow away.

You sally in the sky.
The power of wind surrounds you.
Riding through clouds still grounded,
spring, soaked with morning dew,
releases your longing heart.

CONSIDER

the poor little creature
running across that white picket fence.

Her little feet
pat-skip, pat-skip, pat-skip
avoid the spaces
connecting slats of wood.

Still she moves
but stays on that fence.

She wants to live in
the contemporary house
pat-skip, pat-skip, pat-skip.

She loves her old home
the one with structure,
history and longevity.

Pat-skip, pat-skip, pat-skip
toward the contemporary home
which has no history.
It's new, modern,
still in the planning stages.

Her feet take her back to her history
across the threshold toward her future.

RESEEDING

My journey begins with my clitoris,
a clandestine receptacle of pleasures,
but I'm without my womb.
Two auras remain, my unborn children.

Cysts create their own universe,
liquid and long. My ovaries
vanish from view.

As reproductive organs disappear,
a butterfly forms, flutters and
ascends to balloon my heart.

My heart beats in a tribal rhythm,
an art of living. I'm re-created
from a mosaic of adjustments.
Landscapes of seclusion unfold my faith.

AN EASY SPIRIT

I was stitched together by the hands.

Full of feet for support
my soles strolled the ground
with fleshy weight of step.

Transcending the loss
of polished shine
rubbed in youth,

I have endured sunrays,
absorbed the rain stains.

Leather worn walking
the boundaries of the earth,

eyes sewn closed to the world,
tongues bound together.

Removed and placed in a box
with the lid lowered.

I am without pace, foot free.

FROM THE LAST MAN STANDING

Bob Simion

Shortly after I retired in 1999, my wife, Mary, suggested we enroll in writing workshops to sharpen our writing skills. We wanted to leave a legacy of our life experiences for our family, relatives and other interested people. The workshops taught various forms of writing, and we had our stories and poems critiqued. I never thought I could write a poem until I tried.

It was difficult at first, as I had always written technical and procedural papers. I was very analytical in how I went about writing. Attending the workshops made me think a different way and started the process of recollection, putting my memories and feelings down on paper. It wasn't easy to express or expose my feelings, especially after being very secretive in many of the things I did in the military. I was sworn to secrecy, and it made me feel guilty about releasing some of the information. There are still some things I cannot reveal. However, after listening to some of the other workshop members, I got over my reluctance. I've learned to write about some of the feelings and experiences I've had without revealing classified information.

Writing brought back many memories from my childhood—friends who are no longer with us, my mother's cooking, long-forgotten sounds, sights, tastes, smells and images—and recaptured some of the experiences I couldn't talk about during World War II.

Try this:

Write about some of your life experiences using your favorite foods from childhood, the tastes and smells. What did you smell cooking when you woke up in the morning? What dinner foods bring back family memories, like chicken stew, crepes, stuffed peppers and cabbage, pineapple upside-down cake? What special foods did your mother make just for you? Is there a soup that reminds you of a story? Make a list of foods and see what personal stories you can associate with each of them. Don't forget to use the five senses (taste, sight, sound, smell, and touch) in your descriptions.

FRIENDS

A father holding a little boy
stands behind mourners
in a cemetery with gravestones
and some mausoleums,
like little houses.

Flowers, shrubs,
a few flags wave
in the breeze.
A bronze casket
covered with flowers
rests above a hole in the ground.

The father tells the boy
this part of the cemetery
is for a group of close friends.
A priest prays, people cry,
others are silent with eyes downcast.

The boy looks around, sees figures
rising like mist from the earth:
men, women and children.
Two men dressed in black seem to float
out of a closed mausoleum nearby.

The boy asks his father who these
new people are that have joined the mourners.
The father replies that he sees no one new.

The misty figures stand silent, weave
in the breeze, then turn and return
to the earth, the two men to the mausoleum.

The boy looks at a large monument
in the center of the area.
He asks his father the meaning
of the words on the stone.
The father replies, "Friends return here."

NIGHT DROP

Europe 1944
villanelle

I float down with a gentle sway.
I look at the deadly earth below,
hope against hope all will be okay.

In the distance another is on his way.
His thoughts I feel I know.
I float down with a gentle sway.

Many others have gone this way.
More will follow that I know,
and I hope against hope all will be okay.

Down below I will steal away,
gather my chute and not be slow.
I float down with a gentle sway.

The black billow above allays,
eases the fear of death below;
I hope against hope all will be okay.

Below waits fear—always.
I will land and not be slow.
I float down with a gentle sway,
hope against hope all will be okay.

ENGLAND—FRANCE 1943

excerpt from a larger piece

Arriving in Scotland during the night, the ship waits for daylight before docking. The following morning I go on deck and see many ships in the harbor. I think, *my God, if the Germans fly in here, it will be like another Pearl Harbor.* They haven't yet, I don't know why.

I disembark and an American officer meets me. He says, "I've been waiting for you. I'll take you to the train station, where you will board and go to London." I am still in uniform and have my .45 caliber automatic and a Thompson machine gun.

"What about the guns?" I ask.

"Keep them for now; you can turn them in when you arrive in London." He drives me to the train station, where I board.

After what seems an eternity, I arrive in London, disembark and another officer meets me. He then drives me to a building where I will spend the night and someone will pick me up in the morning. I'm dead tired and settle in the bottom bunk. I am alone in the room and look forward to sleeping. After thinking that, I hear the sirens go off. The Germans have decided to bomb again. This top bunk should protect me, hopefully, from falling plaster. After another sleepless night, I realize our building has not been hit.

The next morning I look out at the street covered with rubble and shrapnel from the anti-aircraft guns. I dress, have a terrible English breakfast of kippers and mash, and wait for my driver. He finally arrives in a Jeep and drives me to a secret base in the country. Here I will receive my final training and orders. I am told that I will be going to France to train the Maquis, the French Resistance Movement, in the use of special miniaturized radio equipment and the Morse code. I know the Morse code but have to learn the use of the equipment.

I am fitted with civilian clothing, which I can pick out. I choose a gray flannel and a brown wool suit. The next day, an instructor drives me to a British airport, where I will receive training in parachute jumping, first from a tower, then from a plane.

The plane is a modified B-24 bomber, a four-engine plane stripped of armament. Training is for daylight drops over the English countryside. The plane has an opening in its bottom, from which I drop like a bomb. At the command, "Jump," I fall out of the plane, count to three and pull the rip cord. I drop, and suddenly there is a jerk when the parachute opens. I float down and try to steer by pulling on the shroud lines, hit the earth and gather my chute. After a few of these, I am ready for the moment of truth, a night jump.

Again in the plane over a specific area at night, I hear the command "Jump." Out I go into total darkness. There are blinking lights in the drop area, which help for judging distance. That done, I receive my final briefing, have my agent radio/transmitter in a briefcase. I also have a training key for practicing the Morse code. My armament now consists of a 9mm pistol, some grenades and, of course, the ever-loving cyanide pills in case the enemy captures me. We've lost a few agents, who were met by the Gestapo, tortured and killed due to leaks in the system or traitors in France. (That is another story.)

The airport is dark, and it's a moonless night when I arrive. I board the plane. Since I am wearing civilian clothes, I put on a jumpsuit, which I will remove on the ground. My cover is that I am a Romanian oil salesman selling specialized oil products from the Polesti Oil Company in Romania, with papers from the German government—forged, of course. Strange, I think, that I am going to France rather than Romania, since I speak Romanian.

We fly over the English Channel and then over France. We have not met any German planes, thank God. I sit, waiting to be told to get ready, thinking of what lies ahead of me. I am told the jump will be a low-level one, which means the drop will be fast.

Suddenly the instructor tells me to get ready. I sit on the edge of the opening, waiting. I wonder if this will be my last time on earth. A member of the crew gives the command. "Jump." I slide through the opening, count to three, pull the rip cord, feel the jerk, and very soon hit the ground. I gather my equipment and in the dim light see some figures approaching. I draw a grenade and am ready to pull the pin if they are not the Maquis.

They approach and I can see they are not military. They come up, hug me and, thank God, speak English, because I do not speak French. We gather my gear and leave the area. We drive to a Maquis safe house some miles away.

I get out of the car, enter the house, and a beautiful young woman called Renee meets me. She introduces me to Pierre, head of the Maquis group in the area. They know why I am here and are anxious to learn how to use the equipment and the Morse code.

I spend two weeks training them to use the equipment and service it if there is a problem. I sent a message in the form of a three-digit number to London announcing my safe arrival the night I landed. We use this type of transmission so that the Germans cannot pinpoint where the transmissions are coming from.

Renee has been a quick learner, and in the process of training we become quite close. Her parents were killed by the Germans as retaliation for the death of one of theirs. They do this by rounding up people from the village and shooting them. Renee has vowed to avenge her parents' deaths.

Training over, the Maquis send their first message to England, and I wait for further orders.

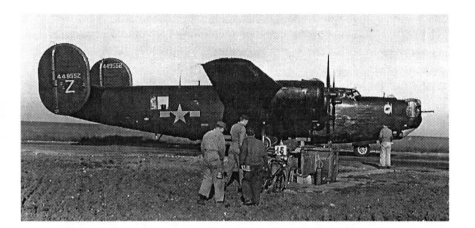

THE MOUNTAIN, NORWAY 1946

It is a snowy January in Copenhagen, Denmark, when five of us—my wife, mother-in-law, father-in-law and a friend—decide to drive to Norway and do some skiing. I have never skied before but am told I will learn while there. I buy hickory skis with Kandahar bindings, which I can use for cross-country skiing as well as slalom by a simple adjustment of the cable bindings. It seems simple enough, but I find out it isn't.

The skis are long. They are fitted by measuring the distance from the floor while I am standing, to the top of my cupped hand while my arm is stretched upward. The edges are lined with steel. I'm six feet tall and have long arms. The skis are heavy. The ski boots are made of leather, like work boots, and are soft enough to be used for cross-country or slalom. The ski poles are bamboo with large baskets for deep snow.

I try these skis on a small slope in the backyard where I am living and immediately fall. I feel like I have two left feet that won't cooperate. I have serious misgivings about skiing on a mountain 8,000 feet high.

I am driving a 1939 Hudson, which has been issued to me by the American Legation in Copenhagen. It has diplomatic plates, which will make border crossings easy. I have military Jeep tires installed for driving through snow. Blankets and a gasoline automobile heater provide heat. Defrosters are electric elements held on the windshield with suction cups.

We fill the trunk with five-gallon Jerry cans full of gasoline, since Denmark and Norway are in short supply. Sweden, however, a neutral country during the war, has fuel—so we can fill our tank there if we need more. We strap our luggage on the roof, but ship our skis to the lodge near Lillehammer, Norway, where we have reservations. We wear our boots.

We start out early in the morning, take the ferry to Malmo, Sweden, and continue north to Norway. We are soon in the foothills of the mountains. It is white and beautiful there, but it isn't long before the driving becomes treacherous. At one point, we stop to check our map at a crossroad. One of the passengers gets out of the car and disappears from sight. The road is sheet ice. Fortunately, he is not hurt from the fall on the ice.

We continue driving through the mountains, blowing the horn at every curve to warn possible oncoming cars of our presence. It is very stressful, since there are no guardrails, and a mistake would end off the road. It is a long way down. We finally arrive at our destination late that evening and are relieved to arrive safely. When we check in and are assigned rooms, I notice that, even though the walk is slippery, the attendant has no trouble walking on the ice. He has wool stockings pulled over his shoes for traction.

In the morning, after breakfast, we get our skis to drive to a slope near the lodge to practice. One thing we have not considered is the morning temperature, 20 degrees below zero Fahrenheit. The car will not start even though we have light-weight oil. We all push the car to the road to start it running downhill. After finally getting it started, I park on a hill with the wheels blocked. Thereafter, every morning, I remove the blocks and the car glides down the road and will start after a quarter mile.

The members of the group teach me how to get up after falling in deep snow, using the large baskets on the poles as aides, also how to brake, slalom and control the skis. I learn how to turn completely around, no easy task with these long skis. I practice for two days before my father-in-law announces we will be going to the mountain the following morning.

We drive to the base of the mountain where we are to ski. We don our equipment and start climbing. There are no tows or lifts. We climb steadily up the side of the mountain. Now I know why the skis have steel edges. Without them, this would be suicidal. Wood alone would not hold up on the icy surface. We climb sideways and forward.

There are trees when we start, which grow sparse as we progress and are replaced by bushes. Then we see nothing but snow and ice. We climb for four hours. I dare not look down, even when we stop to rest for a moment. Looking down could result in fear and over-caution.

At last we reach the summit. The view is of an icy wasteland broken by a stone hut built as a shelter to use if snowstorms come up, which can happen without warning. We eat our lunch while we rest and prepare for the run down.

My father-in-law instructs me to sit down if I can't control my speed and watch out for crevasses, which are dangerous. He warns me that the worst thing that could happen would be to lose a ski. He didn't tell me all this before we started or I might have thought better about going up the mountain.

The run down the mountain is exciting, with a few sit-downs and falls, but I make it. The run takes only twenty minutes. A four-hour climb for a twenty-minute run. The remaining three days we spend cross-country skiing, which is a lot easier. The Nordic scenery is fantastic with snow-laden trees everywhere.

People say that Norwegian children can ski before they can walk. This is obvious from watching them ski so easily. I am envious of their ability, especially after I split my pants when my skis decide to go separate ways.

Thirty years later, I am skiing with short skis (three footers) without poles, enjoying the day with my young son here in Michigan, at Pine Knob, and remembering that first experience of long ago.

360 DEGREES

In the distance he hears someone shout, "INCOMING!" His body feels the shock of the impact. His eardrums seem deafened by the explosion. Someone yells, "MEDIC!"

He wakes in the hospital, people bustling about. A nurse asks, "How do you feel?" He tries to answer, but he can't speak. He hears the nurse say, "You are lucky, no vital organs hit, just multiple wounds." He drifts off.

• • •

At age five, he wakes to gunshots followed by screams and the noise of a car speeding away. The next day he hears that a roomer next door has been shot because he had sex with someone's wife. The victim never walks upright again but is bent over as if in pain.

At age six, he contracts chicken pox. He stands naked on the bed and the doctor tries to touch him. He screams in pain.

• • •

Half conscious, he feels someone bathing him and gently tending his wounds. Someone says, "He'll be better in a few days." He drifts off again.

• • •

At age ten, he sits on the couch in the living room. He waits for the doctor to come out of the kitchen. He can hear the doctor say, "The cauterization wire on the gas stove is hot enough." His mother screams—a crude medical procedure happens on the kitchen table.

• • •

He is aware of moans in the night as he drifts in and out of consciousness. He opens his eyes and sees many beds in the dim light. The occupants are all bandaged, some with partial limbs, sightless or sitting up in bed—the band of brothers. He moves his arms and legs. His limbs respond.

• • •

At age twelve, he remembers the Orthodox funerals in the neighborhood where mourners push the coffin on a gurney through the streets to the house of the deceased. After the wake, a photographer takes pictures of the mourners and the open coffin.

•   •   •

A month later, the doctor discharges him from the hospital. The war is over, and he is on his way home.

In a few years, he graduates from the university and obtains a good job with a large firm. He marries his childhood sweetheart. They have three children. When he finally retires, he receives a gold watch at the office party.

•   •   •

As he walks through the neighborhood one night, a stranger approaches, pulls out a gun and asks for his money. As he reaches for his wallet, the gunman shoots him. He falls clutching his chest as blood flows between his fingers. He thinks he hears someone say, "INCOMING."

EYES

we have seen so much
in our eighty-plus years,
first our mother's smile
as we feed at her breast,
then as we grow up,
our many friends
in the neighborhood,
our teachers in school.

The soup lines
of the Depression.

We learn from the many
books we read in
school and libraries.

We enjoy the thrill of flying,
watching people who look
like ants on the ground.
We are shocked to see
pictures of Pearl Harbor
in newspapers and movies.

In WWII, we go to
the European Theater
and see the whole show
that follows the war
to end all wars, WWI.
It doesn't. What went wrong?

We see many different countries
and cultures during four years
in Europe, much destruction,
death, loss of friends.

After the war, we stay in Europe
for two more years. We

get married, then return home
to go back to school.
Eyes, you are very important.
I couldn't do it without you.

After four years we graduate
and go to work full-time. We
have a family that you watch grow up.

Other wars follow,
but we are only
spectators at home
watching and reading.

We see many political changes,
some good, some bad.
We learn again
many politicians do not
fulfill their promises.

As our power declines, we
wear glasses to help us see.
What we see is a world
still messed up.

PANTOUM FOR THE TELEGRAM

Telegrams have disappeared.
No more singing telegrams.
Will we miss them?
Usage has dropped dramatically.

No more singing telegrams.
Some of us will miss them.
Usage has dropped dramatically.
E-mail replaces telegrams.

Some of us will miss them.
What will become of the machines?
E-mail replaces telegrams.
E-mail is faster—no personal delivery.

What will become of the machines?
Will non-computer people get messages?
E-mail is faster—no personal delivery.
What else will become obsolete?

Will non-computer people get messages?
Cell phones can send text or voice.
What else will become obsolete?
Will ESP become popular?

Cell phones can send text or voice.
Telegrams often scared people.
Will ESP become popular?
Some still use the Morse code.

Telegrams often scared people,
like the fear of a military visit.
Some still use the Morse code.
Communication is becoming high-tech.

Still that fear of a military visit.
Obsolescence is built in.
Communication is becoming high-tech.
Telegrams have disappeared *STOP* Goodbye *STOP*

IMAGE

The face staring at me
in the mirror is not
the face I remember
from years ago.

I question
the image I see, wonder
who he is, this six-foot
figure who's changed so much.

I seek to recall
things I have seen,
horrors of war,
loss of parents and friends.
Many years of working.

Now I remember
love of my wife,
joy of children, grandchildren.
The busy days of retirement.
A time of contentment.

A TRIP THROUGH AIRPORT SECURITY

In 2003, our children in California give us a round-trip ticket on Northwest Airlines to visit them over the Christmas holiday. We pack our bags—careful, as instructed by the airline, not to include in our carry-on baggage anything sharp that could be used as a weapon, such as scissors or a nail file.

At curbside checking, the attendant asks the usual questions, whether the bags have been out of our possession at any time and whether anyone has given us anything to carry on board. We answer, "No," to all his questions.

Since we have electronic tickets, we get our boarding passes in the lobby from the machines set up for this purpose. Once we've done that, we approach the security gates. There the attendant asks for IDs and tickets. After we show those, we approach the metal detectors, place our carry-on on the conveyor passing through the X-ray machines. My wife goes through the metal detectors without a problem.

I have earlier removed all coins, wristwatch, keys, and belt with a large buckle. I have even worn pants with a plastic zipper. I've had problems before, and I don't want a recurrence. I pass through without a problem. I notice the extra security force of armed National Guard troops nearby. The inspector asks some passengers to step aside so he can scan them with hand-held units. In the waiting area, before we board, a voice announces that there will be more random searches. Again we have to show IDs, tickets and boarding passes. The inspector asks one well-dressed man to open his carry-on baggage, which he then searches. He scans the man again and asks him to remove his shoes. He is a first-class passenger. Once he passes inspection, we all board. The flight is uneventful.

When our visit is over, we pack and drive to the San Francisco airport. Again the curbside checker asks us the usual questions, and we answer "No" to all. He accepts the unlocked (as requested) baggage to be checked through. At the security gate, we present IDs and tickets for inspection. We are ready to go through the metal detectors again. This time, however, I've worn the belt with the metal buckle, even though my wife advised against it.

Smart me. I said it shouldn't be a problem. The minute I step into the detector, the alarm goes off. The armed guards finger their weapons and the inspector asks me to step aside and raise my arms.

The inspector thoroughly scans me front, back and sides with a hand-held unit and then asks me to sit down and remove my shoes. I wonder if foot powder is dangerous. He places the shoes into an explosive detector and shortly returns them.

At that point he sets aside my carry-on luggage and opens it. Security searches the contents and finds some very small scissors. I thought we mailed them home with other purchases we made. I explain that they were purchased in England during World War II. Security gives me the option of losing them or mailing them home. I choose to mail them. This means I have to leave the security area, purchase a padded envelope, buy some stamps and mail the package. I do this all hurriedly and then go out of the airport to find a mailbox.

When I re-enter the security area, my belt sets off the alarm. Security asks me to step aside and scans me. Security says I may proceed. A passenger asks my wife, who has been waiting patiently, if I am her husband. She pleads the fifth.

Again, at boarding, a voice announces that the inspectors will make a random search. No one challenges us, and we proceed to board. The flight is uneventful. Next time, I will listen to my wife.

We retrieve our bags and drive home. While emptying our checked bags, we discover that the metal tabs for locking the bags have been destroyed, even though the bags were never locked. In addition, a note inside the bag gives a phone number to call if there is a problem. When I call the number, I discover it is a porno number which describes various sex subjects that I can order and discuss.

The following morning, I call San Francisco Airport and complain. They request a copy of the form, which I mail to them. I never hear another word from them. So much for security.

TWO OF MY LOVES

I fall in love with her immediately.
She is standing in front of my
friend's house and wearing a black coat.
She is beautiful.

I know she is taken,
but I can hope.
She waits there patiently.
I have to have her.

I talk to her lover,
ask if he will give her up.
He says he will, as he is
interested in another.

I say I will take her without pause.
We are together for three years,
have a wonderful time.
However, she has expensive tastes.

One day I meet her sister, who wears a red coat.
I fall head-over-heels in love.
We leave together, spend three more years of bliss,
see the sights of Michigan.

When she travels, she turns many heads.
Her voice is mellow and tuned.
Everyone is envious and wants her,
but she is true to me.

I'll never forget my *MG TD, Mark II.*

CREPES

During the 1960's, I watch my mother when she is cooking and write down some of the recipes of things I particularly like. One that I think is awesome is a dessert called *cletete* in Romanian, crepes in English.

I ask her to make some again, so I can write down how she makes them because I know they are special. She makes a list of the ingredients she needs, and I go to the local grocery store to buy them: regular milk, Gold Medal flour, vanilla extract, eggs, Crisco oil and lard.

I purchase all but the lard, for which I have to go to a Romanian butcher shop about a half mile away. My mother says it has to be the real stuff, not the pre-packaged type. I enter an old fashioned store, where I notice the wood floor is covered with sawdust. I order one pound of lard. The butcher scoops out the amount, places it in a paper container and wraps it.

When I return with the purchases, my mother, wearing her ever-present half-apron, takes out a large bowl and adds sifted flour (2 cups) and eggs (2), stirs the ingredients with a wooden spoon, and then slowly adds milk until the mixture flows like cream, no lumps. Then she adds a touch of vanilla and continues stirring.

She uses a large aluminum frying pan (it will be years before someone invents non-stick pans), places it on the stove and adds some lard and oil to coat the bottom. She adds some batter, which hisses when it hits the pan, and she quickly swirls it to make a thin round pancake-like form.

When the bottom browns, she turns the crepe, lifts one side and adds a little oil, continues frying while moving the crepe in a circular motion. When it is ready, she removes it and places it on a plate. This procedure continues until she's used all the batter. She then spreads some strawberry preserves, which she makes in season, on each crepe, rolls it and places it on another plate.

Sometimes she uses other fillings. When she has rolled them all, she places them in a warm oven until after dinner. The aroma of cooking makes it difficult to wait. I eat them by hand if I can't wait, or with a knife and fork.

Just thinking of them all these years later makes me want to head for the kitchen and start stirring.

AS A CHILD

I remember my mother's garden—
green bush beans
prickly cucumbers
sweet corn
carrots
asparagus
plump strawberries
apricots
red grapes
sweet yellow apples
peppers—green, red and yellow.
The beautiful pansies and roses.

As I crawled
among the plants,
I could taste the Big Boy tomatoes,
my mother's delicious meals,
the warmth of her love.

MARCH NOTES

The yard is still covered with snow.
I see bird and rabbit tracks.

Sparrows squabble.
Blue Jays sound an alarm.

Chickadee heads bob up and down
as they split sunflower seeds.

I am busy keeping the birdfeeder full.
Annie, our new cat, watches from the window.

Suddenly alert, she sees a red squirrel.
Bad news for us; they vandalize.

It's Monday, the postman is late.
He must be bogged down with junk mail.

The weatherman predicts more cold and snow.
Hopefully, April will be better.

The birds are getting frisky.
A sure sign of spring.

THE LOST HILL
terza rima

I gaze across the lake
at trees now barren of leaves,
exposing houses I would not take.

Bare roofs, bricks and eaves
do not a pretty picture make.
It's trees we grieve.

The birds who once sang us awake
no longer conceive.
The hill looks fake.

Empty nests the birds now leave
and floodlights take their place.
It's birds we grieve.

Floodlights expose the barren hill
where once we watched the whippoorwill.

TROUT FLY

Take a dry fly hook.
Fasten in a fly-tying vise,
as if in the mouth of a fish.

First wind the hook with
fine black thread,
then a peacock herl*
circling the body
with its iridescent glow.

Add a bit of squirrel tail
sticking out behind.
Tie in an olive-colored feather
to be its neck.

When tied to a flyline
and cast into a stream,
it looks like an insect
that has fallen in the water,
struggling to escape.

At the far end of the flyline,
attach the fisherman.
Hope that the lure
will fool the wily trout.

*herl: a single peacock feather filament

A DAY IN THE PARK

Susan Kehoe

I like to blame the kids for my re-entry into the world of creative nonfiction after years of writing business memos and reports for corporations. Tricia and Mark want the stories captured on paper because my life is marked by unusual circumstances and unexpected outcomes. They want something more than the oral history about Great Aunt Ollie, who ran a local Pennsylvania newspaper and invented the groundhog legend "… to put Punxsutawney on the map." They want to know what their grandparents were really like, what actually happened, and how it felt to me as a child. They want everything written down so my story won't be forgotten.

My contributions in this section are memoirs, which I define as *writing down what I remember the way I remember it*. Memoirs can vary from each person's vantage point, from the adult to the child, from the participant to the onlooker. Most of my family members are gone, but these stories are my slant on the images and sound bites that linger in memory, a scattering of stories from childhood as well as some recent experiences. Memory has its own stories to tell.

Try this:

Draw a map of the first neighborhood you remember. Include all the details. Ask yourself questions such as: What distinguished your house from others? Were there scary or forbidden places? What were the boundaries you had to observe? Where did your friends live? See how much you remember.

Search for defining features such as brick sidewalks, dirt roads, or a school around the corner. Now write a story about when you lived there, using present tense verbs, as though it's happening right now. I used this exercise in the story, *Crossing Forbidden Streets,* and the process helped me recall what I was thinking as I walked to the corner, what a different appearance the neighborhood had from the other side of the street, and what cigarette smoke looked like coming through a doorway. It helped me create a place that no longer exists the way I remember it, a place my children won't find if they visit that neighborhood today.

CROSSING FORBIDDEN STREETS

Mom tells me to get my father out of the corner saloon. She says it so casually I just keep walking, pretending not to hear as she folds clothes on the dining room table.

"Susan!" Her greenish eyes focus to a steel point. "It's across the street from Lawson's, where you get the milk and bread." Half-gallon bottles of milk carried from the corner are cheaper than home delivery. I'm seven now, so it's my job to run and get whatever's needed. Being good means not dropping the slippery, cold milk, but it has never meant going to the saloon before today.

"But I was just going to do the dishes." Mom loves it when I volunteer for this job, so I use it to stall.

"I'll do those. Go to the corner and get your father," she bargains, "but don't take Dennis." My little brother, Dennis, is lying a few feet away under the tall cut-away buffet that balances Mom's treasured set of Papal plates. He's steadily kicking against the bottom of the buffet, as if daring us to do something about it. Usually I take him with me when I walk somewhere, to give Mom a break from the nightmare of constantly watching an out-of-control child with Down's syndrome.

Mom stops folding Dad's underwear and looks at me with an expression that pleads for help.

On my way to the saloon I stop to examine the edges of a newly erupted brick jutting from the sidewalk. I know the tilt of every brick so I can zigzag around the uneven ones when I roller skate. I peek sideways to the street, hoping to see Dad's two-tone Buick drive by, even though it's unlikely. The shift at the steel mill ended two hours ago and it takes a long time to drink beer. Mom and I never know for sure what time he'll stagger in.

Sometimes Dad yells, though never at me. Last week he came in without saying a word and made slow, crooked steps through the narrow living room, headed upstairs to sleep it off. I hoped nothing would happen this time. At the bedroom steps he stopped, seeming to discover Dennis for the first time, and kicked him where he sat cross-legged laughing at the Howdy Doody Show. It made Dad lose his balance and grab the banister. His mouth twisted and released a low guttural sound. He knelt there, as if in prayer, before continuing up the steps. I held my breath. Dennis crawled under the piano. Mom lit up another Raleigh and ran her hand through her hair.

As I look at the saloon on the other side of Route 8, cars race past. The saloon is next to the corner Texaco station where we buy gas. It's a square brick building with one door and rows of glass block windows that distort the people inside. The saloon has no sign and I wonder how people know where to go. This is the place though, because Mom pointed it out when we drove home from church once. It seems weird that Dad's saloon is across the street from our neighborhood, instead of far away where bad things happen.

Before today I wasn't allowed to cross this four-lane street. At the last flickering of the green light, I close my eyes, run through the crosswalk, and find myself standing in front of the gas station. I hear the Bedford bus whoosh to a stop where I stood a minute ago, just like any other day. From this side of the street, everything looks different. Lawson's is an island surrounded by weeds. My house isn't as big as I thought, and the buckeye tree tilts away from it, toward the sun.

I take the few steps to the saloon and wonder what it'll look like on the inside. I wonder how I'll find my father. And what he'll say. Inches from the door, it swings open with force. A puff of smoke blasts out. For a moment I'm standing at the portal to hell.

I watch myself running through speeding traffic, back down brick sidewalks until I'm safe on the porch step under my bedroom, staring at the buckeye tree and wondering when it will drop its prickly fruit.

A DAY IN THE PARK

Mom begins a fervent crusade to make Dad stop the beer and attend the 1956 St. Pius X Parish picnic at Geauga Lake Park. Both of these things have to happen together, stopping the beer and going to the park. It's the critical step in Mom's campaign to become the President of the Council of Catholic Women. She's bored with being co-chair for the Ways and Means Committee. The unwritten law for the presidency says you have to be the mother of a devout, church-going family. We are not. Not even close. People know me from the elementary school where I'm in fourth grade and my little brother, Dennis, is well known as the kid with Down's syndrome. But no one has ever seen Dad.

"He has to work every Sunday," my mother explains with a martyr's sigh. Even though it's not true, in the blue-collar neighborhoods of Cleveland, it's an acceptable excuse for missing Mass on Sunday. But this is different. Mom understands that in a church where eating meat on Friday is a mortal sin, winning the Council presidency means pulling a show-and-tell with my father, if only for one day. And she pulls off a miracle; she makes Dad promise to stop drinking and go to the park for the sake of the Council of Catholic Women.

The four of us set out on that day with great expectations. The annual picnic is the yearly highlight because kids get to wear pedal-pushers and Keds instead of uniforms. I look forward to a fluffy cone of pink cotton candy and all the rides. The big attraction is a huge wooden roller coaster that makes noise throughout the park as it hurtles above the ticket pavilion. My favorite ride is the Tilt-a-Whirl, which also has a noisy wooden floor that sounds like a roller-skating rink as the wheels run in the spiral tracks. If you pull back on the ride's handle and lean in a certain way, you can get it spinning out of control until everything is blurry.

At the park we walk in uneasy circles in full view. Dad pushes Dennis in a baby stroller that confines him, and Mom greets people like a politician. I just stand there, wondering if anything is going to happen.

I feel like breaking free and running with my friends. Dad is probably as anxious as I am and decides we should try the roller coaster. Dad's pretty nice when he's sober. He buys a whole string of ride tickets, not just two, and I run for the first car, drunk on the prospect of all the fun those tickets will buy. But when the ride starts, the slow ascent is steeper than I remember. I can't see anything in front of me. Near the top I change my mind. I want to go back down—not over the edge. But the ride drops headlong into an abyss.

I let out a hopeless scream. My father puts his arm around me tightly and says, "I've got you."

When the ride stops he keeps his arm around me. "I used to have to hold you down on this ride when you were little," he said. I didn't know that he took me on rides when I was little. "I couldn't keep you in this seat the year you were four! You bounced around and loved it. I was afraid you'd fall out because you were so light and little, but you had no fear then." He sort of laughs. "What happened? When did you get afraid of the fun?"

I guess I look too scared for more rides because soon my father finds the beer tent and orders several rounds, breaking his two-week hiatus from sin. Watching him drink at the wooden picnic bench, I wonder if this is all that happens in the corner saloon. Just solitary time measured in bottles. I watch him drop headlong into that place he goes. Mom's afraid to get him. He'll hit her, but he never hits me. After several attempts, I coax him to leave with us, stumbling in full view of families who seem to freeze in place as we pass. Mom cries all the way home in the car. I don't think she's crying for herself, or for the loss of the Council presidency, or even for the fact that my father has lapsed again, but for lost possibilities. I find myself floating on the ceiling of the car, running away from myself, then to myself, then away again.

REFLECTION ON SPIDERS

Today I realize for the first time that I have to descend the creaky basement steps and find the ironing board without running into any spiders. The cement feels surprisingly cold on my bare feet, but stepping on a spider would be worse. My mother died last week, so now I have to iron my own blouse to wear with the school uniform. It's my first day back to eighth grade since the funeral and everyone will be looking at me in funny, sideways glances. Last week some of the kids from my class walked all the way to the funeral parlor after school. I didn't expect to see them—they looked peculiar standing with coats and books amid the lilies and velvet drapes. Like strangers caught in the wrong place. They didn't talk to me; some of them don't ordinarily talk to me at school. The nuns must have made them come—or their mothers, who wanted them to think about how lucky they are not to be me. After a while they took a holy card and disappeared. Most of their mothers came to evening visitation. It looked like a meeting of the St. Pius X Council of Catholic Women.

There was a short service at the cemetery. I remember how the rain trickled down my glasses while I stood there. The ground was half frozen so there was no hole yet. Nothing indicated that this wasn't an outdoor gathering at the wrong time of year in stark, dreary weather. Rain pooled around neatly shaped tombstones barely visible from the grass. "Makes it easier to cut," my Dad said. I don't remember much else, not even who took care of Dennis. That was one of the oddest parts of all this, not having to take care of my retarded sibling. Everyone calls Dennis "retarded," but he has Down's. He's my responsibility because my father is always working or drinking and my mother was always sick or going to church meetings. Our best thing is walking to the library on Saturday. Dennis behaves because he knows we'll go to the M&M Dairy afterward to get a hot dog and drink at the soda fountain, although the last time we were there the owner made us sit in the back booth. We didn't care; we laughed and made fun of his bald spot.

The librarians aren't too keen on Dennis's weekly visits, either. Sometimes he's a little rough with the picture books. And he wants to take more than three of them home. But they love me. I'm what you call a bookworm. I read with a flashlight all night long and Mom pretends she doesn't know. I guess I'll keep reading in bed now and no one will notice.

The morning Mom died, Aunt Lou came over and gave me a beautiful china alarm clock that plays *Theme from Moulin Rouge*. March is the wrong time of year for gifts. My birthday is in December. She probably thinks I need help getting up for school now that Mom won't be here with the orange juice. Every day Mom hand-squeezed fresh oranges, added sugar and a little warm water to take the chill off, and brought it to my bed in the tin measuring cup. Sometimes I could hear the spoon banging the sides as she stirred in the sugar. Orange juice in bed is magical.

The morning Mom died, people filled the house. Dennis sat under the baby grand piano sucking his thumb and Dad sat at the kitchen table drinking coffee and smoking packs of Raleigh's. Aunt Lou offered to take me shopping for an "appropriate black coat" for the funeral, but I didn't go. It seemed irreverent to go shopping when my mother was dead. I think the day should be treated like Good Friday, fasting and grieving and keeping silent. As soon as St. John's and Sons took Mom from the bedroom, her stepsisters went upstairs to sift through her closets and jewelry. I went up to say something, but was shocked to see my aunt modeling Mom's favorite dress. Last year when Mom was sick with cancer, I accompanied this aunt on a cross-country train trip to California, apparently to see if those relatives would take me after Mom died. I was a disaster the whole trip, desperately homesick and a picky eater. My aunt was furious when I didn't finish my corn flakes in the smoky Chicago train station. It was the wrong place to be eating corn flakes.

I burn my finger trying to iron the pointy collar on my uniform blouse. Maybe you're supposed to iron the collar first? It doesn't matter. Regardless of how I look, nothing will be the same. I step over a spider and ascend the creaky basement steps.

WORKING GIRL

As I leave the YWCA early this morning, I see a girl who looks to be about eighteen taking one last drag on her cigarette. She looks at me curiously, one contemporary to another, while stamping out the butt with her sleek stiletto heel. Her garters peek from under a tight leather skirt complemented by an apache-style pullover. A small, sparkly purse dangles from a long chain; bracelets bangle like the sound of coins in a collection basket. For a second I see a flash of recognition in her eyes, warning that she is my twin. She turns to go home for sleep while I start my walk down Prospect Avenue.

I have the remains from the $50 I won in the Bishop Hagan Essay Contest, minus the bus fare from Villa San Bernardino Convent. I don't feel guilty about keeping the prize money instead of turning it in to Mother Superior, as was the policy. I knew they wouldn't help; they wanted me to stay and become a nun. You were expected to live a spiritual life which they defined as no money, no possessions, no television, and no outside news to distract you from the God thing. They already counted me in their ranks because I was the most unlikely to make it on my own. I was the girl with no mother, no father, and no visitors on Sunday. They knew I had no chance—but I didn't know.

My new home is the YWCA on Prospect Avenue, a major artery in Cleveland full of stores and office buildings. My dad used to say, "If you can't find a job in Cleveland, there must be something wrong with you." So I stop at the first *Help Wanted* sign posted in a window. The woman says she doesn't want *summer* help, which must be what I look like. At the next place I lie and say I want a full-time job with career opportunities—even though my primary goal is to obtain a scholarship to college by September. My mom used to say, "A college degree will make you independent so you don't have to find a man and marry." Right now I just need to earn money to keep going.

But this manager doesn't think I'm a good career prospect, either. Business establishments don't hire people with prior experience in scrubbing floors and praying. There's little call for naming the twelve apostles or telling stories about saints. It's better to know how to run a cash register.

After several more attempts with the same results, it's noon and I'm tired and hungry. There's a Kresge dime store nearby where my mother and I used to stop for a hot dog between shopping trips to May Company and Lord & Taylor. Sometimes Aunt Lou treated us to lunch at the Moulin Rouge Cafeteria when she worked at the phone company. It had a giant windmill on top like the place in Paris. I felt very grown-up there, sliding my tray along

the shiny rails and selecting my own food from the cafeteria offerings—
usually a mound of mashed potatoes and chocolate milk.

As I gobble a hot dog at the Kresge counter, discouragement seeps into my
thoughts. I'm served by an overweight waitress with a ruffled handkerchief
stuck in the pocket of her pink uniform. Like my twin this morning, she
doesn't seem much older than I. Life in a trailer park with an unemployed
man, sprawled on a sofa drinking Black Label, unfolds in front of me.

From the window I spot a large bank on the other side of Prospect and
decide to cross and inquire. I enter through huge, hand-carved doors and
step onto marble floors that seem to belong in an old Roman forum. The
ceiling is high, creating a hushed echo like the sound in the public library. A
long row of tellers stand sentinel at brass-enclosed windows. There's nothing
to do but get in queue and ask.

"Hi, are you hiring? I'd really like to work here."

The teller looks me over. Apparently I look like I just stepped out of *The
Sound of Music*, with puffed sleeves adorning my baby-doll dress. Miss
Kaprowski is probably not much older than I, but wears makeup, hoop
earrings, and has a beehive hairdo. She chews gum and I wish I had a piece.
"You'd have to talk to Mr. Hill, the manager. Do you want me to call him for
you?"

Mr. Hill walks-runs a nervous pace toward the teller cage. He's a small
man with a ring of stiff hair circling his head like Julius Caesar's crown. With
surprising formality he invites me to sit down across from him at an
obsessively clean, ostentatiously big desk. When he sits and folds his hands, I
notice that blue veins run through them like the bus routes going in and out
of the city.

"Mr. Hill, I'd really like to work for you at Cuyahoga National Bank. I'm
looking for a career in banking." The lie seems convincing as it tumbles from
my lips.

"I'm terribly sorry, but we're not hiring for any position at this time."

I hear the faint tinkle of bangle bracelets from the streetwalker; I see the
waitress handing me a pink uniform; I hear my father saying …

"But Mr. Hill, you don't understand. I *need* this job. I have to have a job."

He looks as though he's heard this before. "All right, but anyone who
works here must take a test."

"I'll be happy to take a test," I say almost jumping across the desk.

He puts on his glasses, pulls the one-page test from his middle desk
drawer and hands it to me. "This is quite difficult, and I'll only give you ten
minutes to complete as much as you can." He rummages in his desk drawers

for something he can't find. "Wait a second and I'll get you a pencil, eraser, and scrap paper for figuring."

As he leaves his desk to retrieve the items, I size up the test. It's all math problems, like the workbook pages my mother used to make me practice during summer vacations. I reach for his fancy pen from the engraved stand and start writing in the answers, doing the math in my head, amazed that it's so elementary.

Mr. Hill returns to his desk with the pencil and scrap paper just as I finish. I hand the page back to him. "You finished this already—in ink? Where did you do your figuring?" He turns over the page looking for scribbled numbers, but finds none. He looks at me astonished. "Let me check this." The answer sheet comes out of the drawer and he conscientiously matches each answer. Without hiding his excitement he exclaims, "You have 100%. No one's ever done that before. Did you really do it in your head?"

"Yes."

Mr. Hill looks at me with admiration. "I'm going to put you right on a teller window. You can train with Miss Kaprowski. When can you begin?"

"Right now would be fine."

The tinkle of bangle bracelets fades and pink uniforms never hang in my closet.

THE SEA OF LOVE

I dream that I'm drowning ... trying to stay afloat as the water gets deeper and colder. I flay my arms to stop sinking and touch a fish with a long, smooth body. It's wiggling harder than I am. It's cold and slippery ... and hairy.

As I will myself awake, the wet sensation doesn't stop. I feel before I see—the sheets are drenched. A filmy odor of perspiration permeates the room. And the fish I am still holding is my husband's arm. I try to see through the bedroom darkness. His entire body is dripping fluids that create a pool around us. Drool froths at his mouth. His eyes are dilated and his arms flap flipper-like as he rolls to an ancient rhythm: back and forth, back and forth.

Adrenaline jolts me out of bed. I'm afraid to know, but I have to know; fear becomes subservient to survival. Medical emergencies are not in my repertoire of middle-of-the-night skills. I can get a good glass of water and soothe a bothered baby, but this? I thought diabetics just need daily shots. No one mentioned this part.

Maybe his system needs sugar. I dash to the kitchen for M&Ms, rip open the bag and leave a path of red, yellow, and green pieces. But George is unconscious. Prying his mouth open to drop in candy is almost impossible. I force some onto his tongue and push his mouth up and down with my hands, to squeeze the chocolate into his body. Red, yellow, and green ooze out the sides of his mouth, making puddles on the pillow. Maybe he needs something liquid that will slide down, a Coke. But when I try pouring a gentle stream of sweet liquid down his throat, he starts to choke, unable to swallow.

His body is shutting down. As alternatives run through my head, I consider how angry he'll be if anyone finds out he's ill. But his body is limp now, no longer fighting or rocking, a rattle emanating from his throat sounding like a death knell. I have to call 911.

"Can you send EMS please, my husband is unconscious." My heart pounds as I try to sound calm and clear.

"Are you at 7777 Lincoln Drive?" a controlled dispatcher asks.

"Yes, it's a condo complex, last building, first unit. Please hurry."

"How did this happen?" *As if I know.*

"He's a diabetic."

"Did he forget to take insulin?" *The person on the line asks the obvious question she must have learned in training.*

"No, I watched him take it when we returned from the restaurant." *How many hours ago was that …?*

"Did you give him more insulin?"

Why would she ask me this? "No, I think he has too much insulin in his system, he needs sugar," I reply with a sarcastic edge.

"Okay, they have diabetic supplies on the truck."

The flashing lights of a police car break through to the murky bedroom within seconds. In my panic I haven't turned on lights. The police officer pounding on the door is peering in the side windows with a flashlight and holstering a gun. He reaches the bedroom in a few strides smashing a red M&M into the sea-foam colored carpet. When he sees George lying in a skeleton-like pose, he grabs something on his shoulder and speaks into it,

"Get them here quick."

"They're turning into Lincoln Drive, they see your car."

The red and white beacon is a lighthouse on the dark road. I think I hear the officer say, "Oh God," under his breath, but maybe it's me.

Four EMS techs and another police officer jam into the small bedroom. The lid of a metal case crashes into the nightstand leaving a permanent gouge.

"He's diabetic," I instruct the paramedic with the long needle. He's focused and doesn't respond.

"What's his name?" A police officer has a clipboard and pulls me to the side. "How old is he? Are you his wife? Can I see your driver's license?"

"He has no pulse," a second paramedic says.

There are many conversations going on. I think I hear someone say something about *no pulse*. That can't be right. My eyes are trained on the paramedic techs, but the officer wants endless information for his form. Doesn't he know I have to be with George?

"How old is he?" The officer wants demographics.

"When did he have insulin last, Ma'am?" the paramedic queries. This question takes priority.

"About seven hours ago, I think, after dinner." *It's my birthday, so I know we had a reservation at our favorite restaurant.*

"Ma'am? His age? Are you his wife?" The officer's questions are relentless.

A long needle goes into George's arm. There's no reaction. I want to be at his side, but there's no place to fit between the medical equipment and technicians stationed around the platform bed. So many people, so much equipment wedged into one little room.

"Give him another one," the boss tech orders.

"Are you sure?" another tech asks. *If the tech's questioning a second dose, do they know what they're doing?*

"His glucose reads 19," someone says.

I know the reading should be around 100. Seventy is the lowest *safe* number, and I've seen George act confused and panicked when descending to that point. How many times I've witnessed him pricking his finger, catching the blood drops onto a thin strip, inserting it into a small meter, and pronouncing a number. My life is measured in insulin needles laid out on the kitchen table.

"Never below 70," the doctor emphasized. "He needs to eat if the sugar level falls below that. Orange juice or a Coke should bring him back up quickly." *No one's told me what will happen if the level drops lower than 70. I never knew to be afraid.*

"Okay, I think we have a pulse."

Watching the process of awakening was as strange as the dream. George opens his eyes with the stunned look of someone who doesn't know where he is. He can't quite speak, his words slur like someone intoxicated. He looks at all the strange faces and calls my name. Without thinking, I step over the back of a kneeling tech and take two giant steps across the bed, dodging tubes and needles, to sink down by him. George grips my arm as if to say, *"Don't leave me."* His eyes are still dilated as he tries to focus, repeating my name over and over like a chant.

The techs ask him questions. "Who's the President of the United States?" George thinks about that and says, "Kennedy." Thirty years too late. Gradually he realizes where he is and wonders why an EMS crew is standing in his bedroom.

"You went into hypoglycemia, buddy. How much insulin did you take?" the needle tech asks.

"Same as usual." George doesn't understand why this has happened, but he's not going to look afraid.

"Well, you better be more careful."

They review his regimen of six shots a day from a mixture of two different types of insulin. He's what they call a *brittle* diabetic. What we don't realize now is that unstable sugar levels are a sign of failing kidneys. Insulin control is jagged as the body moves to changing rhythms, shifting and unpredictable. George's condition will worsen until we find ourselves sitting for hours in dialysis, his name on a list with thousands waiting for a kidney transplant. But that is still a few years away.

In the interim we keep a Glucagon Emergency Kit in the scarred nightstand, a fast-acting injection for our visits to the sea. I consider the pebble-like M&M stains on the carpet a triumph over that night and the nights that will follow. But the terror never quite leaves me, a recurring dream in my catalog of fears. I find myself living on the edge, wondering every night if we will be swept out to sea.

INVOLUNTARY SEPARATION

I hear sobs from behind the closed office door. The administrative assistant stationed across the room ducks behind the computer screen. The manager and employee have been in there less than a minute. Another manager stands waiting by the door holding a brown cardboard box in each hand, while I sit in a plastic and chrome chair, a throwback from the 60's when this company was in its heyday. The manager with boxes is called the *guide*. His job is to escort the terminated employee back to her desk, collect her company badge, pack her personal belongings into the cardboard boxes (making sure she doesn't access the computer), escort her to her car, and watch her drive off company property.

The rest of her work group has been sent to a dummy meeting to prevent embarrassment and long good-byes. But one late arriving employee, Glenda, enters the office and asks, "Where did everyone go? Did I miss a meeting?" Before anyone can answer, she hears the sobs, glances at the boxes, and probably puts two and two together. She may be experiencing that split second before a car crash when you realize that danger is speeding toward you and there's nothing you can do. Glenda flees into the hallway, a long braid of red hair dancing down her back.

The assistant looks at me and says, "She's next. I wonder if we should have her hang around." Terminating people is as strategic as any military tactic: a surprise meeting, a sealed severance package presented by a strange manager speaking from a script, an outside consultant, such as myself, to calm the person while the manager escapes. Involuntary separation is meant to be a surprise attack. Ideally the ex-employee is off the premises in twenty minutes and can never re-enter.

Suddenly a new round of desperate sobs resounds from the office. "Do you know the emergency number for the medical people in the command center?" I quiz the assistant. She's probably worked here for thirty years and looks surprised that there are medical professionals waiting for emergencies. Or maybe it's the idea of a *command center*.

Most people don't understand the physical effects of shock in an involuntary separation situation. Everyone's on edge because of yesterday's critical incident. A man in the Research Department snapped when he heard the news; he ran out of the meeting room and kept running around and around the hallways. Maybe he thought if they couldn't catch him, they couldn't fire him. Security finally tackled him.

The sobs grow louder and I walk toward the assistant. "If I put my head out the door, please call this number. I don't want to wait if she needs medical attention." One time an employee reacted to the termination speech by lying down on the floor in a fetal position. He made an eerie, animal sound, but the manager kept talking, determined to finish the speech.

Suddenly it seems quiet behind the boss's door—ten minutes have passed, much longer than the allotted time for this part of the process. The manager slinks out the door and beckons me in. It's my job to ensure that the employee is in sound condition before leaving the building. My personal mission is to point her to the future, give her an idea of the next steps toward career transition.

"Hi, Carrie." Her eyes are bloodshot and she has several tissues wadded up in her hand. "I'm guessing you've had better days ..."

"What am I going to do? How can I make my house payment?"

"That's always the first thing we think of, isn't it? Our obligations rather than ourselves." I'm not sure she's hearing me. "You're going to be okay. Health benefits are still covered through your husband ..."

"Oh, my God! I hope they don't fire him, too!" Her voice escalates. I've been briefed that her husband works in the same department.

"Who knows what's happening. They might fire him, too!" Even though her separation is due to downsizing and job eliminations she calls it *being fired*.

"He's fine." I know they're keeping him, although married couples are occasionally both released at the same time. "Let's think about you right now."

She responds to this idea by dutifully reviewing her work assignments. "I have my project list on my desk. I'll have to explain it to whoever takes over for me," her voice drifts in thought. "It'll probably be my cube-mate, Glenda." It won't be Glenda with the red hair. She's next in line for involuntary separation.

"I don't want you to think about work right now. You'll be going home in a little while and I wonder if it's better for you to take a taxi."

"Oh no!" She interrupts. "The neighbors can't see me coming home in a taxi! That's too embarrassing." She pauses, "This whole thing is so humiliating."

"Yes, it is." Validating the emotional reaction is critical to her acceptance. She takes her hand from her eyes and regards me more seriously.

"What if your husband drives you home?" Terminated employees don't realize that they must exit company property within minutes. I'm convinced it isn't a good idea to let her drive.

"No!" She gasps. "He'll be so disappointed in me. And he doesn't want to be disturbed." The idea of telling anyone is beyond her coping ability at the moment.

She looks at her freshly manicured nails and admits, "I don't think I should be alone right now, either. But I can't go home." She remembers something else. "This will kill my father! He had a heart attack when my brother was laid off two months ago. And now it's me." She sobs quietly. In this city, it's common for generations of a family to work for the same company. It's a badge of honor. Family members may have worked here before her—without getting sent home in a taxi.

"You were under a lot of pressure in this job. It may have been a bad fit for your talents and personality. There are other possibilities, industries with a different philosophy." From the look of interest on her face, I think we might be turning a corner.

"Do you think anyone would hire me? I'm forty years old, for God's sake! I've been *here* almost twenty years. I don't think I can *do* anything else."

"There is quite a bit you can do. Your skill set is transferable to other industries. There are growing companies hiring for your talents right in this town." Most people never think about options outside the company they work in. Of course, it could mean a dramatic change in lifestyle or relocation to another state. "You were smart to get your degree through the tuition assistance program. Everything is on your side. You may not see it this way, but the career that's ending is great preparation for your next one."

"Maybe." She shakes her head. "I saw something interesting in the want ads yesterday. Maybe I just need a good resume."

"A resume will be easy to put together with your rich experience. Employers see many people changing jobs mid-career since the 9/11 tragedy," I offer. "People are beginning to realize that life is too unpredictable to work twelve hours a day doing something they don't love."

We nod in agreement.

Note: This story is not about a particular person or place. It is developed from a variety of experiences throughout my entire career.

COLOR ME ELECTRIC AQUA

We wait at the top of the basement stairs stuffing lambs wool into the points of our shoes and criss-crossing pink ribbons around our legs. The class before us finishes the lesson and disbands, tromping up the stairs where we wait. Some of the six-year-olds try to balance glitter-covered pillbox hats on their heads while others fuss with ruffle tutus and drag loops of sequins. In an instant we realize the costumes for the May dance recital have arrived.

"What are you going to be?" Louise is the first to ask a chubby dancer who hunts for her coat in the small, jammed landing. The theme of the recital this year is candy, but no one knows which candy she will symbolize until the costumes arrive. That's Miss Eileen's way of keeping our attention.

"Gumdrops," the smallest of the group answers. "But my hat doesn't stay on." As if to demonstrate, the hat falls from her head, sprinkling green glitter across a scattering of saddle shoes.

"Don't worry," Louise reassures her with the air of a recital veteran. "Your mother will sew an elastic strap to go around your chin and the hat will stay on for the whole dance." These beginners don't do much more than point their toes, put their arms above their heads, and turn themselves around. A lot like the hokey pokey. Our class has already graduated from soft flat ballet slippers to pointy toe-shoes that raise us to a new level. We know with confidence that Miss Eileen has saved the best candy—and costume—for us.

"First position, second position … Louise, knees straight, toes *out*. Remember girls, a graceful rise," Miss Eileen sings as she demonstrates. We practice barre exercises in a line across drab linoleum tile. Five black turtleneck leotards reflect in the mirrored wall while LP records drop onto a turntable. We practice our dance routine twice, including Miss Eileen's solo, before she reveals the secret. Finally she lifts the handle from the record player.

"Girls," Miss Eileen asserts, "You will feel very sophisticated in the costumes I've chosen for you." We gather around, waiting for her to reveal treasure.

"For this year's recital," Louise grabs my hand, "You have the honor of being … the M&M candies!" Miss Eileen is triumphant. Louise squeals. And all I can think of is *Melts in your mouth, not in your hand.*

As if she sees my fears, Miss Eileen reaches into the shipping box and slowly unfolds a long chiffon skirt, the kind that floats after you wherever you walk. It's a beautiful color, something between blue and green. "Each of you will be a different color M&M. Susan, *aqua*." She hands me the skirt. I see that it ties on with a grosgrain ribbon and has an uneven hem, longer in the back. This is a real ballerina outfit.

Next, she presents the headpiece. As Miss Eileen waves it above our heads, the cap seems to be made of tinsel from a Christmas tree, but it's not silver. This tinsel shimmers in an aqua color. Even under the raw basement light bulbs, it reflects in millions of dazzling pieces. It looks like *electric aqua*. It might have been stolen from the set of an old movie spectacular my mother likes to watch.

Miss Eileen continues conferring colors. "Mary Kay, uh, fuchsia … no wait, orchid would be better on you. Louise, fuchsia … and Sally, saffron. Carla, this sage will be lovely on you." Just like that, the colors are determined.

This is the best costume I've ever had. Everyone's thrilled except Louise. When it's our turn to climb the stairs she grumbles, "I never saw a *fuchsia* M&M. What ever happened to red?" At the top of the stairs where the next class waits, our glittering caps catch their attention. The tallest ballerina whispers to Louise, "What candy are you going to be?" Louise ignores her and huffs off to find her penny loafers, but I whisper back, "M&Ms!" The wide-eyed ballerina makes a silent, clapping sound.

It dawns on me that red is not as mature as fuchsia, just as blue-green is simply not the same as aqua. It doesn't matter that in 1959 there's no such thing as an aqua M&M. Blue is crayons. Aqua is the new world.

• • •

Waiting backstage in the high school auditorium on the day of the recital, I'm more curious than nervous. Louise prances up on her new toe shoes looking at me. "Aren't you worried?"

"About what?"

"Doing the dance right. I've had nightmares I'll mess up on that tricky part when Miss Eileen starts her solo." She looks like she really needs me to agree, so I say it worries me, too, although, it hadn't occurred to me. I know my part by heart.

I hike up the invisible elastic on my strapless leotard and glance out front at the sea of parents buoyed to their seats, my mother among them. The gumdrops are just finishing their routine, shedding a trail of glitter from safely secured hats as they march in clumsy circles around the stage. My number is next and the last in the recital. I notice Miss Eileen stretching in preparation with her leg warmers crunched around her ankles. She dances as the sixth person with us, but somewhere in the middle, steps out and performs her solo. We become a chorus line for her sixty seconds of fame.

Too suddenly the bright lights shine in my eyes and the audience goes black. The music from giant speakers jars me into the familiar routine. Part of the way through I'm so caught up in the flow that I forget myself and step into the spotlight with Miss Eileen for her solo. I execute the first difficult step in perfect time with Miss Eileen, as if I'm her shadow. Pink pointy shoes fly across the stage, arms become graceful wings, and chiffon flows as if it's enchanted. But on a pirouette, I spot my colleagues in the background. My heart does an arabesque. I can see Louise's eyes telegraph disbelief on my second rapid spin. *What was I doing out front with Miss Eileen?* Just as suddenly as I began and without missing a beat, I find a way to dance backward and melt into the M&M lineup.

The dance ends without another glitch. We take our theatrical bows and parents shout "*Bravo! Bravo!*" Miss Eileen gathers flowers from admirers and all the dancers come on stage, all the candies together in one giant stomachache.

When the curtain comes down after an eternity of applause, I run backstage and hide while the other dancers join their parents out front. Clearly I can never return to dance class. Worst of all, I'll have to face my mother. She'll be profoundly disappointed in me.

I wait in hiding until most people leave, not wanting to run into Louise or any of the dancers. I wish my aqua costume wasn't so obvious and I remove the tinsel cap just as my mother spots me. She's approaching with a wonderful, broad smile.

"Sweetheart, you didn't tell me you had the lead in the dance!"

I'm speechless. I try to recover, to say something clever about a surprise for Mother's Day, but I burst into tears. "I messed up, Mama! It wasn't my part! I ruined everything!"

Now Mom's confused. "No you didn't. It looked like part of the dance," she says, putting her arms around me. "People thought it was beautiful. You're the only one who knows it wasn't planned that way."

"Well, Miss Eileen and the dancers know ... Do you really think the audience didn't see that it was all wrong?"

"No, it was wonderful! I'm so proud of you."

Mom was right. No one ever said anything about spoiling the dance, even Miss Eileen. And the following year, Miss Eileen included in the program a *Me and My Shadow* dance with another student dancer.

Just as aqua isn't blue-green, I learned that things don't always appear to others the way they appear to you. I *have* entered the brave new world.

BLUE CANARY

Polly Opsahl

Paint Pictures with Words

Words fascinate:
the rhythms they make,
feelings they trigger,
pictures they paint in the mind.

Take a blank page; blacking its
whiteness with inked words,
create a kaleidoscope
of emotion, color, sound.

Take words in, taste
the bittersweet, feel
the sting, hear the thunder,
watch them heal, let them
paint stories in your heart.

When my mother passed away in 1994, I found myself just wading through my days—work, sleep, work, sleep—for what felt like a year. I had always written, mostly stories, and dreamed of a novel someday. When I felt the need to do something, anything, to change the dragging of my days, I signed up for a creative writing class.

I entered that class with an *I don't do poetry* attitude and haven't stopped writing poems since. Writing words in patterns of rhythm and sound, finding boundaries in lines on the page, gave me an outlet for the mix of feelings I had concerning the losses in my life. It helped me find again the good memories and not just the sad ones.

My mother had many tragedies in her life. She buried two sons. She taught me that despite sadness—or maybe because you never know when it is waiting around the corner—you need to enjoy life and find the beauty in every day. It's out there beyond the blue.

 Try this:

Sit by yourself somewhere: your backyard, a restaurant, your living room. List thirty things that catch your eye. Review the list. Pick out twenty items that have a connection to something happening in your life. Arrange them in an order that makes sense to you (opposites, similarities). Find the rhythm and rhyme in the words you noticed (see *Great Lake Shoreline*).

BLACKBIRD ON A POPLAR BRANCH
for my mother

It's a beautiful day.
A cool breeze caresses my bare legs,
carries the sweet scent of honeysuckle.
I hear a fish plop within marsh grass
that lines the rocky shore of Forest Bay.
A single red-winged blackbird perches
in a dead poplar. A fly buzzes past.

Another blackbird lands on the tip
of the tall, feathery grass and sways
back and forth, back and forth.
Late afternoon sun warms my shoulders.
It is peaceful here

and yet it's not.
There is a low roar of leaves in the wind
like pages of a book fluttering open
on their own in a horror movie.
Seagulls fish in the distance:
a few harsh cries, a dive, a silver
fish plucked from its life,
just like you were taken from mine.

And yet it's still a beautiful day.
A cool breeze caresses bare legs.
A fish plops within marsh grass.
A single red-winged blackbird
perches in a dead poplar.

SUNDAY DRIVE

Whenever I'm in the car,
hot summer sun baking the dash,
I'm transported back to 1960's
summers and Sunday drives
in my dad's Ford Fairlane,
a Tiger game on the radio.

Baseball, Ernie Harwell's, *long fly ball
to left field*, turns my stomach a little
since I often get carsick
with the mix of stops and starts.

Six of us smushed on two bench seats
before air conditioning comes standard,
little girl, middled by older, sweaty bodies,
tries to see out the window, not knowing
where we head, this family minus one,
older brother dead for years already,
killed by the machine that cages me,
and still we drive—past the herd

of Shetland ponies in Meadowbrook fields,
over Paint Creek at Avon Park where cool shade
calls me, on to Mt. Avon Cemetery to put
Mother's purple irises on the graves of her father
and son. Finally allowed out of that moving prison,
I dance around gravestones, careful not to step
where I know bodies lay beneath, soft
breezes caressing the freedom of death.

CURTAINS FALL

My daughter carries her perfect tulips
in a plastic grocery bag, lays them
next to my mother's pink headstone.

It's my mother's birthday
and right on schedule
my daughter pulls up in her
Mustang convertible, and I jump in.

I call her car *The Blue Blur*
because she drives like Jackie Stewart
and my mother. We race
down South Hill, as Mother waits.
We'll get in trouble if we're late again.

September heat hangs heavy
like sheets my mother nails
over the archway as curtains
to separate our part of the house
from Grandma's. I feel the slow
pull of time as I watch those cotton sheets,
thick as memory, come down
when Grandma breaks her hip.

Mother sleeps in Grandma's dining room,
wakes suddenly in the night when
Grandma cries out.
I remember her words,

I'm here, Mother.

GONE

in response to a painting, "The Upstairs," by Charles Sheeler

She is gone;
the flimsy attic door hangs open
and she is gone.
I cannot bring myself
to pass through and climb those steps,
those curving wooden steps,
to taste the reality
of emptiness that waits above.

She is gone for good this time.
Those times before, she threatened to leave,
and leave she did then, too,
but always she came back,
always before because before
the attic door stayed closed,
closed and locked
and locked it held her secrets,
the secrets she could never reveal.

I knew about the shoes,
dancing shoes wrapped in pink tissue.
I knew about the letters
from her lover in New York,
the letters tied with green ribbon,
and I knew when he left her
to taste the damp scent of tears
when she slept and wept late into morning.

I knew I could never hold her
like the frame on the wall
now empty of her picture couldn't hold her,
as if she slipped its wooden confines,
slipped out the unguarded window.

THE ABC's OF FRIENDSHIP

What is a friend? A single soul dwelling in two bodies. Aristotle

Almost from the beginning I knew you would
become a true friend, one who stayed through
catastrophes and celebrations as well as the
day to day just plain living that can be so boring.
Everything about you was new at
first. But now, after all these years, we have
grown to be two parts of a whole,
halves of one mind. Sometimes, we think so much alike
I wonder how it's possible and then, we
joust on charging steeds at each other like
knights, where only one can win, so the other must
lose. We hold tight to opposite positions.

Maybe we were lovers in another life,
now destined to be together in some
other partnership. Being friends can be more
pure than being lovers. There is a tension in love, a
quality that doesn't exist between
real friends. *Does he love me enough? Could there be
someone else?* With a true friend, it's always enough.
Thousands of *someone elses* won't
undermine the friendship. You can show a friend your
varicose veins, the age spots on your hand, the
way your butt has begun to sag,
x-rays of your liver showing spots of cancer.

Your friend won't take off in her
Z-28, race to leave you, zip around curves,
zoom through traffic lights to get away from
you because she thinks you soon will be
x-ed out. A friend takes you
wig shopping, and tells you to pick one that looks
vampish. She buys scarves to wrap your bald head,
underwear to make you laugh when you go for chemo
treatments every day. A friend reads to you,
sits by your bed, holds your head when you

retch because the medicine, like
quicksand, drags you under, makes you weak.

Perhaps this is why we were meant to be friends.
Only God knows what's in store for us beyond
now and maybe that's good, too.
Maybe if I had known how hard it would be to watch
life drain out of you, see you fade every day,
keep this vigil, I would have feared
jumping into the battle, too scared of the pain
I feel watching you go. People say
how good a friend I have been to you,
giving my time and energy, caring for a dying
friend. But they don't understand.
Eventually, cancer takes the best of both of us,
dear friend. But that's not true either. You having
cancer allows us both to be our best. You, while
battling death, show great courage, and I show love
as simple as kissing your stubbly head goodbye.

YOU'RE STILL MY BEST FRIEND
for Tammy

and it's been two years since you died, two
blue years where words aren't as
clear as they used to be, and they
don't rhyme, and my dreams are darker
even than my worst nightmares and more
frightening than your diagnosis. With you
gone, peppers taste pale, and bees can't find a
hive where they can make honey.

I don't want to get out of bed some days,
just roll over, pull covers over my head,
keep my door locked, pretend 1999 never happened—
lousy, lame, loathsome 1999. You
might still be alive if we could have jumped to
now and skipped '99 and 2000. Scientists have

only just discovered some molecule they
plan to test on melanoma by year's end.
Quite simply, it might have saved you,
rid you of the horrendous disease that
sucked the life out of you, robbed me of
the best friend I ever had. And here I sit,

useless, unable to move forward, trapped in a
void of vacant days and variable dreams,
wondering where you are—hopefully in some
Xanadu where there's no cancer, where
you can laugh and dance on two whole feet in the
zenith, where someday we'll sip chai latté together again.

CHRISTMAS BLUES

I'll have a blue Christmas without you.
Elvis Presley

At first, I don't realize what's happening.
Blue has always been a color for me, not a
condition. Another holiday season begins,
dreary and dull, because you, gone these two years,
eight days, are not here to sing carols with, eat
fruitcake with, laugh with, shop with or buy
gifts for. When I hear that first, *Bah-*
Humbug, and realize it's from me,
I wonder if I'm getting the flu, or maybe I
just didn't get enough sleep last night. I
keep making excuses, refuse to see until,
like the proverbial light bulb, it pops into my
mind that the anniversary of your death
nears. I went to our office Christmas party
one night and found myself sitting alone.
People were dancing and drinking. It was
quarter past nine, and I wanted to be home.
Rightfully, you should be here, not ashes
sprinkled on a beach in Florida.
This third Christmas of grief, like waves, drags me
under. I try to keep myself focused, but my
vacant horizon blurs. Blues run together,
waves and wind, sea and sky, love and loss.
X marks the spot on the treasure map of hope,
yet it keeps changing places. I think I'm almost there,
Zap! it's somewhere else. I'll keep searching.
It's out there, beyond the blue.

THE FINAL COURTESY

From the earliest origins of amateur radio, hams have sent one another
postcards ... which serve as a confirmation of contact over the air.
Harvard Wireless Club Website

Ham radio operators reach out over waves,
connect with strangers in other lands or down the street.
An NPR broadcast highlights a hot August night
and the usefulness of this antiquated method of communication,
when the power grid failed and the cell phones died.

A postcard, the final courtesy from
a conversation with General MacArthur
sent years ago still hangs pinned
to a nostalgic ham's bulletin board,
an acknowledgment of a connection,
however fleeting, that still holds,

like in the movie, *Frequency*, when
a young man lost in an everyday world
of conflict and confusion happens upon
a connection to his past—a conversation
with his long dead father. In the way

of movies, it happens. The past
changes and the present is
resolved. The son saves the father,
so the father can save the son

and the reality of you, my friend, not
so long dead by comparison—is filled
with the wish for the missed conversation.
Your cancer the static that broke our connection.

POSTAL BLUES

I'm blue, postal blue
from my baseball cap with its *Eagle in Flight*
going nowhere, to my stick-to-your-back-in-the-summer,
doesn't-absorb-a-drop-of-sweat polyester shirt
with red and dark blue pinstripes,
even darker blue ink stains over the pocket
where I forget to click my pen closed
and mark my shirt forever,
to the oh-so-slimmingly vertical
navy braid trim down the outside
on my uniform slacks,

to my white cotton socks
with dark stripes at the top,
circling my ankles like shackles,
to the stained blue heels of my once white socks
where my feet got soaked in last Tuesday's storm
and my black (or so I thought) walking shoes
that can withstand pressure to the I-don't-remember-what degree
bled into air-breathing/moisture-absorbing/
100% cotton, no longer white

white. I'm blue, postal blue—
my feet hurt,
my back aches,
my hands cramp
from holding millions of letters
over thousands of days
between every other finger
so tendons stretch
until they almost pop.
I can't hold on any longer.

THE CAT WAITS

I pull into the driveway after another
late night at the union office.
My family forgot, again,
to leave the porch light on for me.
As I drag myself from the car,
cross the motion sensor beam,
garage lights click on
illuminate the path almost
all the way to the front door.
The cat waits under the blue spruce.

I'm home from a poetry reading,
and the living room TV reflects
off the front window. I see
the shape of my daughter's head
as she finger-combs her long hair,
fluffs it dry so she can go to bed.
The cat waits under the mountain ash.

Rain pours over my car, as I park
outside the garage, remember
my husband gets to park inside
because it's *my* opener
that has stopped working, and it's
my mother's furniture taking up
half the space. The cat watches me
from the back of the rocking chair.

Sun glares off my hood ornament,
I slam on the brakes to miss
bikes scattered like pick-up sticks.
Home from work before dark
thanks to deliberate effort
and the effects of daylight savings time,

I walk in the front door, imagine
my family's thrilled surprise.

A stream of teens flows past:
Hi, Mom, bye, Mom. We're
going to the movies. Dad called.
He'll be home late; see ya.

The air tingles as kids ride off.
I feel I've wandered onto a movie set
after all the actors have gone for the day.
The cat's nowhere in sight.

IF I RUN AWAY TO THE CIRCUS

Maybe I'll be a tiger or a lion.
I'm fairly well-behaved, but what
fun to roar my displeasure
whenever the mood strikes.
If the ringmaster takes a wrong step,
I'll bite off his head.

I can be a clown with curly
orange hair, a purple nose that honks
when children squeeze it. I know how
to hide behind a mask
to keep everyone else happy.

Maybe I'll be the high wire act.
Heaven knows I'm used to dancing
a straight line, keeping my balance
through dips and turns of life,
wondering who really hopes I make it,
who waits to see me fall.

I think I'll be a trapeze artist,
fly high above the crowd,
never touch the ground,
and catch myself, always,
when I let go.

IT SEEMS INNOCENT ENOUGH, PUTTING THE KIDS TO BED

First the blanket rumples, crawls
up my legs, growling and nipping.
Then the little clowns start to fade
in and out of the wallpaper,
skitter on all fours like spiders
in white, ruffled clown suits,
three black pompoms down the front
and rickrack edging the ruffles.
They have red ball noses and snarly red lips.
Pointy teeth snap sharply. And then

the fake Barbies attack, suddenly life-size
with torpedo bosoms and fly-away
hip-length hair that winds its silky strands
around my throat as they fall on top of me,
stiff and unbendable. They have startling
blue eyes, thick slashes of shadow over
spiked lashes and red, permanently
heart-shaped lips. Their unblinking eyes
stare into mine as the pressure gets heavier,

heavier. The only way to save myself is to
grab them by the hair, rip off their plastic heads.

WHAT HAVE I DONE TO MY DAUGHTER?

We both prefer the newest glasses
purchased last summer on sale at Target,
the ones with houses of Provence
circling under a pale blue sky.

My daughter and I sit drinking tea
at the Holly Hotel and discuss
the order in which we select our
drinking glasses from the cupboard.
I have told my husband this daughter
is his because she and I are so
unlike each other. I am surprised
to find we have this connection.

Our second favorites are blue goblets
the color of my father's eyes—
the grandfather she never met.

She tells me she drinks water
only out of glass, not plastic.
I say I'm the same. She once
measured how many ounces of water
each kind of glass holds, so she would
always know how much water
she drinks. The blue ones hold more
than the ones with the houses.

I tell her my next favorites are the tall,
green ones or the clear nubby ones
my husband bought at ACO for a dollar.
She says she won't use those,
won't drink water if they're all
that's left in the cupboard.
I ask about the dark green ones
with the grid (like graph paper) design
on the side. I bought them because

I thought she would like them. She tells me
she drinks only orange juice in those.

We laugh together at our mutual
idiosyncrasies as we sip tea—
hers Lemon Delight in bone china,
mine Earl Grey in a stoneware mug.

BLUE CANARY

I see a blue canary and think: *sky*
before my mind can turn the color gray,
as life so hurried, hectic passes by

on little sleep. The gentle summer nights
will rush like blurs of cars go by, the way
I see a blue canary and think: *sky*

is where I'd like to be with you, so why
can I not make the choice to slow, to stay,
as life so hurried, hectic passes by

astray? I do not, cannot make the time
for you, for friends, or even time to pray.
I see a blue canary and think: *sky,*

a special place to lift my arms and fly.
This insubstantial time will end one day.
My life so hurried, hectic passes by.

One day I'll wake and wish that I had tried
a little more to make the best of days
I see a blue canary and think: *sky—*
my life, though hurried, will not pass me by.

SACRED

Love me as if I were a small speckled feather.
Feel the curve of my spine. Run your fingers
down my sides and back again.
With the right touch, I will mold myself
to you, but move wrong and I will arch away.

Kiss my thirty-three freckles, each one, twice.
Hold the small red stone of my heart
in your hand, feel the shape of it, know
my scars as if they were your scars,
see pieces gone missing, some tiny slices,
others chunks the size of teeth marks.

Respect me as if I were Niagara Falls,
an exhibition of nature's beauty.
Feel my power, the thunderous rush
as millions of water droplets crash over rocks,
emotions churning beneath the surface.
Treat me frivolously, and I will send you
over the edge, a shattered, oaken barrel.

Cover me in rags; put me on display.
I will stun you with dialog, seduce you
with song, dance a *cha-cha* in your veins.

Cherish me as if I were the last three
buttons in the world. One, small and white
to wear on your shirtsleeve, one brown
and strong enough to hold your wool coat
closed against winter's cold, and one so fragile,
it can disintegrate like spun sugar.

GREAT LAKE SHORELINE
Forest Bay, Lake Huron

A quick, *wheat, wheat, wheat, wheat, wheat,*
crunch of sticks, rustle of sea grass,
wild Siberian irises—three yellow, one blue with a ladybug,

five/eighths of a clam shell, some driftwood,
the two-pronged track of deer in the mud,
a toad, a longer, *bleet, bleet.*

A log in the tide rocks, almost making it over
before it plops back where it started,
like a baby trying to turn over for the first time.

A swallow scolds, *you're out too far, you've gone too far,*
one y-shaped log, sun-bleached, the color of seagull feathers,
foam at water's edge, froth on a cappuccino.

The wind hums, paper rattles,
eight goose feathers—one snatched by the wind.
With a loud *splash*, a fish jumps so fast there's only a ripple.

Two sticks rub together like children
bumping against each other and away,
laughing before they bump together again.

Tall grass sways and bends, bows
to an audience of dancing wildflowers,
little pink ones, and forget-me-nots,
always forget-me-nots.

WHAT THE DIRT AND I REMEMBER

Bernie DeHut

"Memories may escape the action of the will, may sleep a long time, but when stirred by the right influence, though that influence be light as a shadow, they flash into full stature and life with everything in place."—John Muir

My husband told me to keep a notebook. It was our epic road trip: six weeks on a motorcycle zigzagging across the U.S. and Canada to Alaska and back. I jotted down a few things: the price of breakfast and cheeseburgers in Alaska, addresses of friends we made along the way. I wrote a bit more in the notebook when I first traveled to Europe, details I found quirky, like an eleven-year-old British boy remarking that his restaurant supper was *lovely*. I thought photos were better than words and bought new cameras for these adventures, but I learned that even slides projected across my entire living room wall couldn't capture the grandeur of the Canadian Rockies or a millennium-old cathedral. So I began to take conscious mental snapshots. I'd reflect, focus on sights, sounds and smells, and recall the way a place and a moment felt. Then I'd promise myself, *You'll remember this*. Those mental snapshots inspired this collection I never intended to write, freefalling into this company of writers and the opportunity to share our stories.

Try this:

What mental snapshots have you taken of places or events? Whether deliberate or accidental, some will surely inspire you to write about them. Just do it and see what flows from your memories. Use details, scrounging for exactly the right words to create a rich, multi-dimensional picture that takes others into your experience. Maybe *Answering the Call of the Wild* or *What the Dirt and I Remember* or *Craving* will help you see how attention to details allows you and your readers to live awhile in another time and place.

ANSWERING THE CALL OF THE WILD

First, you wild thing wanna-be, go to motorcycling class, where guys and gals wearing boots and leather and friendly determination will teach you to scan, identify, predict, decide, and execute. To slow, look, lean, and roll on the throttle. They'll teach you that sooner or later, you absolutely, positively will fall down, and to dress for the occasion. They'll encourage you to try again and again even if you do stall the bike thirty-seven times until your hands and feet learn to cooperate and roll into first gear surely and smoothly every time. They'll teach you to ride like you're invisible, plan your escape routes, and anticipate the worst-case scenario, like a stupid driver in a van running you off onto the shoulder of the turnpike, with no awareness of your presence. They'll teach you to trust the bike.

Shop carefully, diligently for the bike you can trust. It will be your only companion a hundred or so miles from a place to fill your gas tank and politely empty your bladder along the loneliest highway, U.S. 50 in Utah or Nevada. It will be your sole support as you lean further into an unexpectedly sharp curve on the Blue Ridge Parkway in Virginia. It will be your only way out of the gravel and mud, away from the bear and the black flies in Northwest Territories.

Choose a bike like you'd choose mountain-climbing gear or a lifetime friend. Choose one that fits like your most comfortable pair of boots or jeans. If it's the right machine, it will feel like an extension of you, your cyborg other half. It will be fast enough to make your eyes water and your spine tingle, full throttle, on a deserted two-lane road between just-planted soybean fields in Indiana. It will be nimble enough to swing easily back and forth through the switchbacks on naked, rocky Beartooth Pass in the Absaroka Wilderness. It will be light enough that you can hold it upright as seawater sloshes over its wheels on the tossing deck of the Cape Hatteras ferry, beset by a freak storm in the Bermuda Triangle. The bike for you needn't be shiny, sexy, or new, but it should make you smile when you see it.

You won't need all those accessories the salesman proudly demonstrates as if he held the patent on each one. They're for poseurs who don't comprehend that all the lights and dingleballs are designed to take you away from the experience of riding, to simulate your daily commute on four wheels. You don't need a sound system; you'll be playing music in your head all day long riding the plains, over and over that catchy tune you heard in the café this morning over eggs and bacon and home fries. You don't need heated seats or electric chaps or vests. You'll dress in warm down and fleece and Gore-Tex layers, and when it gets too cold, you'll smile ecstatically over a bowl of chili at that place in Zoarville, Ohio, giving the waitress an especially generous tip. You won't need a trailer for all the stuff you'll learn you don't really need to take with you anyway. You don't need helmet speakers to chat with your buddies because riding isn't about talking. It's about seeing, feeling, soaking up, inhaling your surroundings, not needing interruptions, becoming part of the road. Let it all in, and you'll be better company when you stop to get coffee or to stretch your legs. You'll listen well to the wistful, weathered octogenarian telling you about the old Indian Chief or Harley he rode years ago. You'll enjoy the company of long-haul truckers who can't resist ambling up to your bike, giving it a visual once-over, and then telling you about the one at home in their garage or imagination.

At first, all your brain cells will be thoroughly occupied with staying upright and watching out for the other guys, because even one of them on four wheels outnumbers you. You'll fret and sweat stopped on steep hills in Pennsylvania, with one foot on the ground and one on the brake, praying you don't stall when the light turns green. You'll be surprised by the draft sucking you in the first time you pass a semi on the highway. You'll feel nervous on the road, and wonder why you ever thought this would be fun. But gradually, after months of miles, you'll begin to relax and enjoy. You'll start waving back to all the other bikers on every make and vintage, who acknowledge kinship as they pass, even from the other side of the interstate. You'll wave to folks on porches. In coveralls and aprons, they'd never wave to a car, but they'll wave to you. Little kids will wave from vans and SUV's, sometimes furtively, but they'll want to grow up to be like you, and that's how they'll let you know. Before you know it, you'll be grinning and waving to cows in pastures, too. Really.

Stay away from the super highways because the same guy built them all, and they make every place look and taste the same, whether it's Michigan or Arkansas or Nova Scotia or Germany. Study the map. Find the back roads. You'll always feel at home there, be well fed and entertained. You can slow down and follow your nose to the best pit barbeque joint in town, or catch the small homemade sign for the Indian rodeo or lobster pound or Firemen's Picnic or Amish homemade noodles. You'll find small towns where locals will tell you anything you want to know, and some things you don't care to. You'll learn that, west of the Mississippi, road construction means first of all destruction, the phase you always seem to encounter. You'll curse and pray riding poorly marked thirty-mile detours, and following pilot cars in slippery chloride-coated, muddy, blasted bedrock work areas. Back roads can be ferryboats, too, crossing rivers and harbors and patches of open sea. You'll find out that insects feel like bullets at cruising speed, especially those monster grasshoppers in North Dakota. You'll be startled by wildlife that graze and hunt along roadsides and sometimes play chicken with you: moose, bear, mule deer, antelope, coyotes, snakes, bighorn sheep, prairie dogs, marmots, snapping turtles, cougars, and a herd of oncoming bumble bees on a bridge crossing the Mississippi.

You'll learn to ride in rain and snow and hail and one hundred-five degree heat and the fringe of a tornado because you'll have no choice. You'll just do it and know you've learned something in the process. You'll seek out the mountain passes because they challenge you and the same café in Miles City, Montana because it comforts you. You'll follow the ghosts of other adventurers along paths still remembered by road builders: the Lewis and Clark, Pony Express, Oregon trails, and Route 66. You'll come to love the wild places, however desolate they appear at first. The fragrance of gray-green sage and the calm of pronghorn antelope grazing will feel like homecoming whenever you ride the high plains, still longing to be a wild thing, but only able to pretend.

TAGGING THE SERPENT

It's a wet and windy Sunday afternoon in St. Ignace, Michigan, and we're stuck on the wrong side of the Mackinac Bridge. When we approached the tollbooth heading south on our motorcycles, we were turned away by the toll-taker with a warning: "Sixty mile per hour winds out there. No motorcycles. Have to wait till it settles down some." We'd seen the wind advisories as we approached the bridge but thought they applied only to "high profile vehicles," like semi trailers and RV's. Kurt tried to argue with the toll-taker, pointing to a motorcycle that had just arrived at a northbound tollbooth. "That bike just crossed; why can't we?" But the fellow just shook his head, and we U-turned.

Kurt is determined to get home today. I'm more flexible; if I have to call into work tomorrow because I'm stranded, it's no big deal. With hardly a day of work missed in over twenty years, it should be no big deal for Kurt, either, so I don't understand his attitude. I suspect it's just his stubbornness; he doesn't take "no" for an answer, even from Mother Nature. He's so determined that we drive out to the local trailer rental shop, which of course is closed. He thinks that maybe we can rent a small U-Haul cube van, load the bikes into it, and cross the bridge with that. How much could it cost for such a short rental? But the place is deserted, and when I go to a phone and call the number, it doesn't forward to someone who answers, as he hoped it might.

Next, we're heading down the road watching for a vehicle or equipment trailer in tow and headed toward the bridge. Maybe we can find someone with room to haul the bikes across for us and rent space on his trailer. We have no luck with that scheme, either.

So we're hanging out in a typical tourist trap restaurant, where we're the only customers on such a dreary afternoon near the end of the fast-fading weekend. We eat mediocre pasta under fluorescent lights while we watch the flags outside yank at their poles. There's no noticeable reduction in their frantic waving while we worry over our coffee. We're weary from the 900 miles we've traveled in the last day and a half, and less than enthusiastic about traveling the 250 still ahead of us in the rain. We rode to Mackinac yesterday just for lunch and a reason to ride on such a picture-perfect summer day. It was so gorgeous, and such an easy ride that after lunch we decided to travel across the Upper Peninsula to pay a surprise visit to Kurt's mom. Now, traveling in the rain with a bad case of biker's "bench butt" and unable to cross the bridge, we feel like yesterday's inspiration was just another dumb idea.

We complain to one another about the bridge authorities' irrational refusal to allow southbound motorcycles to cross, while northbound bikes continue crossing without incident because there's no one to stop them on the south end. Ever since that Yugo went airborne and flew over the railing into the straits a few years ago, there's been much more attention to safety, or at least to maintain an illusion of safety during periods of high winds through the use of electronic advisories and weather information channels posted along I-75 and US-2. But we've been across the five-mile-long bridge dozens of times on two wheels and four, in all kinds of weather conditions, and we aren't easily intimidated.

Our usual reaction at first sight of the bridge from the hill near Seashell City is one of happy anticipation because it means we're northbound and possibly westbound on vacation, if only for a weekend. If we can see the bridge from that distance, it's an exceptionally clear day, like yesterday. Often, we don't see the bridge until we round the curve near Miami Beach Road, and sometimes the two suspension towers are completely engulfed in fog and clouds. Temperature varies dramatically across the five-mile span: it generally feels twenty degrees cooler in the middle than on the southern approach. Some days that's refreshing; other days it's freezing. At night, the suspension cables are lit by colored Christmas lights, best viewed from one of the scenic lookouts along US-2 or on one of the glossy postcards available everywhere. The bridge is a marvel, not a threat. I've driven my motorcycle on the metal grating in the inside lanes when maintenance work required it, wobbling along as if possessed by a tremor, and even that wasn't so bad.

Boredom and tension haul us out of the restaurant and onto our bikes. We want to be home before dark. We'll head to the tollbooth and see what happens. *Hurray!* There's a new shift on duty, and the man takes our money. Then he tells us to pull over into the line forming to our right; we're to be part of a caravan. The caravan is the bridge authority's attempt to control motorists in windy conditions, with semi trucks and large RV's assigned to the outside lanes and smaller vehicles theoretically snug and protected in the inside lanes. But there are no semis and RV's today. Just wimpy two- and four-wheeled vehicles. We pull into line and wait for the pilot vehicle that will lead our paranoid procession across. With each passing minute, I grow more anxious. I remember the snake.

During my freshman year in college, the psychology instructors encouraged us to participate in advanced students' experiments, so I signed up for one. Part One of the experiment took place in an upstairs lab in the dark and ugly Chemistry Building on a dreary winter day. I sat while the senior student explained what we'd do that day. Across the room was an aquarium with a fair-sized snake in it. I was told it wasn't poisonous and was virtually harmless to humans. The senior would walk me through several actions and record my self-assessed fear level after each step. I started by looking at the snake in the aquarium across the room. Then I moved closer in stages until I was standing beside the aquarium, each time telling the student how fearful I was on a scale ranging from *Not at all afraid* to *Very afraid*. I had little to no anxiety until the moment I donned thick leather welder's gloves to prepare to touch the snake. Its head was up and alert to my presence alongside its glass apartment. Then I slowly reached into the aquarium and gently touched its mid-section with a thick-gloved finger. Its head veered away suddenly, startling me into heart-pounding, adrenaline-rushing fear.

I was part of the control group that would receive no training with the snake, so I was done with my participation in the experiment for a month. I made up my mind early that next time I'd skip that last step. When in Part Two of the experiment I declined to tag the serpent, completing one less step than in Part One, I asked the senior whether my behavior was consistent with that of other control group members. "Well, I'm really not supposed to tell you anything because the experiment isn't complete, but your behavior is pretty typical," he responded. I wasn't surprised. Why would anyone repeat an action that triggered the visceral fear response?

My eyes refocus now. There's a guy in a uniform walking along the bridge caravan line, shouting into the wind. We strain to hear our instructions as the rain starts to fall again: *form a single line, keep to the inside lane, and travel at a speed of fifteen miles per hour.* You need only have ridden a bicycle to know that stability on two wheels requires momentum, and you don't ride any kind of bike across wet metal grating like that in the inside lane if you can avoid it. The bridge authorities are obviously clueless about motorcycles, and I'm not entrusting my safety to them. Kurt and I agree: to hell with the caravan.

We get moving and creep slowly south in line with the other vehicles for a hundred yards, then accelerate into the outside lane, which we have all to ourselves. It turns out we need the whole lane for our aerobatics, as we try to keep ourselves and the bikes upright in a fierce sixty mile-per-hour crosswind. A seventy-five mile-per-hour wind would be categorized as a hurricane. Kurt's bike in front of me is at a sixty-degree angle to the pavement, and I'm sure mine looks the same. Whoa! The first turnout acts as a windbreak. My bike abruptly veers right, and an instant later left, where I'm back in the wind again. I adjust my position in the lane so that the next windbreak doesn't cause me to veer into the traffic on my left or the bridge rail on my right. I'm approaching the north tower, along with a slippery suspension joint on the bridge deck, at about thirty-five miles per hour. I pass under the tower and control the accompanying involuntary right and then left swerves. I've no idea whether there are freighters in the channel to my right or tour boat rooster tails off to my left. I don't notice whether the towers are visible; my eyes are glued to the road in front of me.

I'm on the middle span when Kurt's brake lights alarm me. "No, you can't slow down out here!" my brain yells to him. Kurt's bike is heavier than mine, a "full dress" model with a fairing to block the wind, and in this case fight the wind. He's struggling. I slow just enough to keep a safe distance between us, applying the brakes as if I were driving on ice. I continue to ride along at a drunken angle, feeling like the bike and I are panting for air. I pass under the south tower. More than halfway there. The home stretch. Just a little farther.

I focus on negotiating the last windbreak, the south turnout. With that and the most violent gusts behind me, it suddenly hits: the rush. Now I get it! This is why people leap out of airplanes and why they sail their motorcycles over trailers full of crushed cars. This is what the trapeze artist feels. I'm flooded with euphoria, a little shaky, and glad to see Kurt's turn signal as we exit for gas at our usual stop, just south of the bridge authority vehicle that's always waiting to transport motorists too frightened to drive across. I've tagged the serpent again, and I understand why.

WHAT THE DIRT AND I REMEMBER

It's been five years, and I miss the West. The one that's still wild, the one few folks know or want, and the one that can be reached only by back roads. The one with the really big sky, the fragrance of sage, and not much of anything else. Where there are few colors, few people, few distractions. Only a mirror that drives most people crazy.

You know you're there when the diner's a café and every town has a *Stockman's,* even if you're still in Minnesota just over the river. The cattle know you; you're a stranger. They look up, curious, and follow your two-wheeled progress down the road with their eyes. The antelope, too, interrupt their grazing, alerted by the ticking sound of your motor. A ranch hand, treating himself to a night on the town, nods at your bike and strikes up a conversation at Saturday supper, where he enjoys steak and you order exotic chicken and salad. You're a topic of discussion at poker later that night and over coffee in the morning.

There are gulches where water once was and cottonwoods that remember. There are large bumps on the prairie, buttes that hold metals and minerals. You can't help yourself as you watch their flat peaks for smoke signals, just like in old movies. There are badlands below the horizon, where you never guessed, and just over the cattle guard, there are big holes in the prairie. One holds a surprise: an oasis, a river. Others are empty silos where missiles took root but never sprouted. A few keep their secrets along with the skeletons of monsters that passed by and passed on. Only the dirt remembers. Camouflage colors, gray, beige, and sage, hide everything but sky and the mirror.

Ghosts of dreams haunt silvered wooden memories of buildings, rough-sawn, hand-hewn, clapboard and log. They wail about trying so hard to succeed at subsistence, no options, no luck, no divine intervention, only trying and dying of trying. Ghosts of travelers call to followers, their neighbors and kinfolk, from outcropping rocks they long ago signed and dated in careful, elegant, eloquent script, craggy guideposts to manifest destiny. They saw hope in the mirror and spent it all to cut trails of narrow wagon ruts. The dirt remembers them, too.

The road is lonesome, no need for stop signs or signals. Only signs reassuring you of comforts ever closer in Belle Fourche, Rosebud, Roundup, Ingomar, Greybull, Guernsey, Red Lodge, Ten Sleep. Wall is special; signs beckon for hundreds of miles: *"Have you dug Wall Drug?"*

There are miles of wire fence where upside-down boots trim the posts. There are miles of no fence and "Stock in Road" warnings. There is stock in the road, a herd you stare down as you pass, wondering if the color red on your bike will really upset the critters. Docile, as if under a spell, they allow you to pass down the road to Enchanted Rock.

Switchbacking, zigzagging, you climb mountains without guardrails, riding into the sky for a hazy view of endless prairie. Harsh, stingy, dry, intemperate. Still you come back year after year. Cattle still graze. Hay fields still grow. Snow fence is thirteen feet high. The stubborn still try. They look into the mirror unflinching.

IF IT DON'T KILL YA ...

Kurt pulls his motorcycle to the side of the gravel road and motions me to ride up beside him. His gesture is that of a scout in an old western, and he looks the part with his long red beard and generous covering of trail dust from head to toe. "I just saw a bear cross the road up ahead, so watch out for it," he says.

"Black or brown?" I ask, trying to get an idea of size, as if it matters. I don't want a close encounter with *any* bear.

"I couldn't tell through all this dust, but it was *big*."

That makes it a three-bear day, so far. First, there was the unseen one who left a large pile of scat fifty yards from our tent during the night. Presumably, it was the same bear for which a large canister trap had been set alongside the service road behind the campground. Kurt didn't tell me about the trap, knowing, after more than twenty years of marriage and camping, I wouldn't stay the night if he did. As it was, the howling of wolves interrupted my sleep and made me acutely aware of the remoteness of this place, and uneasy about camping in a park that was all but deserted at the height of summer tourist season.

Bear number two was a black cub hunkered down alongside the road this morning. We stared at one another as I rode slowly past, trying to keep my adrenaline in check while I wondered where its mother was.

Now, hours later, I'm in no mood for an up close and personal bear encounter on this unbelievably awful road.

The journey, a detour, really, started two days earlier at a crossroads in Alberta. We were on our way to Alaska, which we'd visited a few times before. But Kurt stopped at a visitor center where he caught the bug to visit someplace we hadn't seen, Northwest Territories. "It'll be an adventure," he said with the enthusiasm of a kid headed for Disney World. For several hours now, I'd been mumbling to myself that what I needed was a vacation, not an adventure.

We crossed the 60th parallel twenty-four hours ago. The weather was sunny and mild, so we stopped to take photos of our old BMW motorcycles in front of the Northwest Territories border sign with its polar bear logo. When we stopped at the nearby welcome center for maps and information, we saw no other visitors, just a young, earnest-looking, uniformed representative of the Territories. Kurt asked him about road conditions on the westward loop that would take us through the southern portion of the Territories and on to Fort Nelson, British Columbia.

"Oh, it's good gravel all the way. You'll have no trouble," the officer replied.

"What about traffic on the road? I mean, are there enough vehicles traveling that way so that we can get help if we have some type of problem?"

"Oh yeah, there's plenty of tourist traffic. You won't have a problem. And there's great scenery and wildlife, too. You should stop at the waterfall just up the road."

"How about gas? Where can we find gas?" Distance between gas stops always requires more attentiveness on back roads west of the Mississippi.

"Well, there's Hay River and Fort Providence. Then there's a store along the road here, near Fort Simpson. And there's gas at Fort Liard." As he spoke, the officer pointed out the locations on the map. They were pretty far apart, but nothing we couldn't handle within the range of our gas tanks.

Our host was upbeat and enthusiastic, very likeable. From the looks of things, he was probably glad for some human company. He signed our "North of 60 Explorer" certificates, and then followed us outside. "Nice bikes," he said approvingly. We thanked him and left with no idea we'd curse him for the rest of our trip, if not the rest of our lives.

We headed north, through country that was neither forest nor tundra, but something in between. It was green, but not terribly scenic. We stopped and took some photos at the waterfall, and then focused on getting to the campground in Fort Providence.

To reach our destination, we needed to ferry across the McKenzie River. I'm not fond of ferry crossings, and the McKenzie was especially intimidating: wide, dark and deep, with a swift current. We parked behind several other passengers, and stood by our bikes to steady them in the event of any pitch and roll. Though the crossing was uneventful, I was nevertheless glad to ride off the boat and onto land on the north side of the river.

We found the territorial park, where only four campsites were occupied. We pitched our tent high above the McKenzie with an impressive view of the river. But we realized there was a price to pay for the view: the continual torment of tiny, biting blackflies. We were glad to escape to town for dinner, away from the relentless insects. It seemed late for blackflies, and when Kurt asked about that in town, the locals told us blackfly season in Fort Providence is basically all summer. That explained the campground's pitifully small population of campers. We lingered over our after-dinner coffee, then explored a bit, stumbling across a sign that posted ice road conditions. We learned the frozen McKenzie becomes a road for truckers during the winter, as do other rivers in Northwest Territories. "Sounds crazy to me," I remarked. "But at least there'd be no blackflies then."

We woke early and were on our way, with the blackflies providing additional motivation to get moving. It was another sunny and mild day, perfect motorcycling weather. The pavement ended at the edge of town, but the gravel road beyond was as advertised by the welcome center guide. We could comfortably travel around forty-five miles-per-hour and admire what scenery there was. There's still a snapshot in my head of one view unique in my travels across Canada and the U.S.: an unbroken vista of evergreen tops as far as the eye could see to the north, a window through the brush on a seemingly untouched wilderness.

The road turned south and conditions deteriorated after our burger and soup lunch in Fort Simpson. The gravel became coarser, requiring us to downshift and slow down. We assumed it was a temporary condition, and that we'd soon find ourselves back on a smoother surface. But the gravel was getting looser and larger, so that it felt like we were driving on marbles. We geared down more, riding in first gear at a maximum of fifteen to twenty-miles-per hour. As promised by the guide at the welcome center, there was quite a bit of traffic. While we never saw anyone who looked at all like a tourist, every twenty minutes or so a truck full of local mine workers would roar past at sixty miles-per-hour or more, raising such a dense cloud of dust, we had to slow to a crawl until we could see again. It was amazing that Kurt saw the large bear that brought us to a stop on the Fort Liard Trail.

We continue on, cautiously scanning around us for the bear, but it's probably long gone, just as anxious as we are to get off the road and out of the dust. After a half-hour or so, Kurt's bike zigzags precariously in front of me, and he stops again, frustrated. "I almost dumped the bike!" That never happens to this guy who's ridden nearly three-hundred-thousand miles in all kinds of conditions, including some very miserable roads in Alaska and Mexico. His complaint gives me some perspective on just how lousy this road really is. Kurt suggests I lead for awhile. I point out he'll be eating more dust, but he thinks it will help if he focuses on me and the horizon ahead.

It's painfully obvious we aren't going to reach our Fort Nelson destination by nightfall, so we soldier on, determined to try to reach Fort Liard, the only other dot on the map. We wobble, weave, curse, and occasionally stop to relieve the tension in our shoulders brought on by our absurd balancing act. We keep expecting that at any minute conditions will improve, but are disappointed mile after mile. If there's scenery, we miss it, since we have to keep our eyes on the road, though Kurt does spot a wood buffalo off to our right. I'm relieved to finally reach Fort Liard with no damage to us or our motorcycles. We look like a couple of saddle tramps with dust clinging to every inch of our riding suits, faces, and bike surfaces.

Fort Liard is called a "hamlet," which sounds much more charming than the remote settlement it actually is. We roll up to the only motel, a shabby, peeling wooden structure perched atop a small grocery store that's closed. It looks like it should be named "Very Last Resort." I ring the buzzer and am greeted by a stoic, middle-aged woman who quotes me a rate of $125 per night. "You've got to be kidding," Kurt says, starting up his bike to head for the rustic campground outside of town. No way is he paying $125 for that fleabag place, but there's no way I'm camping after the day I've had. "I'm paying for it!" I growl. Kurt decides there's no point arguing and sulks as we carry our bags up the rickety stairs.

The room looks like a decorator's 1960's nightmare, with dirty orange shag carpeting and phony wood-grain paneling, but it has a shower and a bed and no four-legged critters roaming in it. Maybe there are some six or eight-legged critters; I'm too exhausted to care. I'm satisfied. After a burger at the one and only restaurant, basically a shack, we're glad to shower and crawl into bed. The funny thing is, we can still see the road coming at us when we close our eyes. Kurt assures me the road will be better tomorrow when we cross the British Columbia border a few miles away. I don't know if it's the darker side of my nature or a genuine premonition, but I'm not so sure.

We're back at the lone café for breakfast in the morning. Then we head for the most attractive building around, a native crafts center. I indulge in retail therapy to compensate for yesterday's miseries, buying beautiful Acho Dene bead and quill work, a birch bark basket, and a bear-shaped pin made of walrus ivory that only aboriginal people may carve and sell. I load my treasures carefully into my dusty red duffle bag on the seat behind me, and we hit the road, heading south.

The sky's overcast and the smell of smoke is heavy in the air, though its source, a nearby forest fire, isn't visible. It rained during the night, so dust is no longer a problem. Sure enough, as Kurt predicted, in British Columbia the road surface does change, though not as he anticipated. We stop to assess a deep mud hole full of water spread across the entire road. We inch our way along the edge of the hole, where the surface appears to be less soupy. We're barely past when a black pickup blasts through the middle of the bog, the driver amused when he throws mud everywhere. Thankfully, the glop misses us.

The road continues to be sloppy as we ride on in the gloom. Kurt has me riding in the lead, so he'll know right away if I run into trouble. That's exactly what happens when the motor beneath me sputters and stalls. My bike slowly lists to the left and then slithers onto its engine guard in the ooze, as the unexpected stop catches me off balance. Kurt stops and helps me get the bike upright again. "What happened?"

"I think I've got engine trouble."

Kurt presses the starter, and the engine responds immediately. No trouble there. He looks down at the front of the bike and finds the real problem: the space between the front tire and fender is completely filled with mud that has the texture of wet cement. The rear tire and fender look the same. The engine hasn't the power to muscle the wheels along against that heavy sludge.

After we scrape the mud off tires and fenders, I climb back on and start the bike. Just ahead of us, the road climbs a hill. What next? Kurt gives me a pep talk, "If you get moving, keep moving till you get over that hill. Don't look back and don't worry about me." I head off, shaky with adrenaline. Somehow, we both manage to keep moving. After we crest the hill, the road surface changes again, finally for the better. We still move slowly and cautiously, wary of surprises, but can relax somewhat and admire both the sights and smells of the thick, quiet evergreen forest through which we ride.

It's afternoon when we finally reach pavement: the Alaska Highway, or "AlCan." Kurt turns to me and teases, "Wanna kiss the pavement?" I curse and shout a frustrated farewell to the damnable road we've just traveled. We turn eastward, heading toward Fort Nelson. Then it begins to rain.

WAY TO GO

It wasn't a near-death experience. No lights, no tunnel, no beckoning presence. Just a Sunday morning mishap. They say, sooner or later, you will fall down. My brain destroyed most of the negatives; only a few photos survived, some accompanied by sound, others mute.

The white line at the edge of the road, the realization, "Oh, shit!" My red motorcycle gas tank all by itself over there in tall grass. His blue motorcycle parked on the shoulder, pointing the other way. Ambulance doors open, apparently for me. Severe pain in my head and neck. "Can't you take this board away?" Then an ordinary urgency, "I need to use the bathroom."

Images lost forever in the coil of ruined film: the rest of my bike, most of that day, the ride in the ambulance (*Did the siren blast and the colored lights flash?*), ER tests and procedures, x-rays and scans and insults to my injuries, the things I don't remember I said that made perfect sense all the while, and whatever went wrong in the first place.

It's a perfect, clear, sunny day in the middle of Nowhere, Missouri: gentle country road; breakfast of eggs, toast and bacon; the bliss of vacation. Until. Perhaps dehydration? Near fatal distraction? A poorly timed nap? A vicious attack? First strike of oncoming disease? Too much curve in a swerve? To avoid what or whom? Nobody knows. *I think I still can look cool when I find that my fragile, red, Ray Ban wire-rimmed sunglasses survived without injury.*

It occurs to me now I could have been finished. It wouldn't be a bad way to go: cruising the back roads with all the time in the world, wind in my face and then making a quick exit. No anguished, painful shrinking and fading. No disintegrating of self and all that it loves and clings to. No need to pack up and move to Oregon for a happy ending. Just "Oh, shit!" The film breaks and then nothing.

FINAL SALE

"You must be Rosie," I greet the short, forty-something brunette, look into a face I immediately like and trust. We meet on a chilly May morning when her uncle picks her up at the airport and drives her to my home and motorcycle stable. We were introduced by eBay a week earlier, when she purchased my vintage BMW motorcycle posted on the auction website. Funny how a shared passion forges immediate bonds; within a minute I feel like I've known Rosie for years. I can tell she's pleased by what she sees: a bike that's exactly as advertised. It's in beautiful, ready-to-ride condition, worth every penny of her winning bid. I'm still incredulous that someone would agree to pay thousands of dollars for something she'd seen only on her computer screen.

Kurt, my husband and the bike's mechanic, recites its history and a litany of maintenance recommendations until Rosie starts asking, "Would you please write that down?" While he finds a notepad and pen, I invite her and her uncle in from the chilly garage into my small kitchen for a hot drink. They both choose herbal tea. We talk about where the bike has traveled: everywhere and back, easily and reliably. We talk about her reasons for flying all the way here from Philadelphia, her reasons for choosing this old BMW. She had a similar one in college, but had to sell it to help pay tuition bills. She describes the last-minute bidding frenzy on eBay, when she didn't know if she'd win the bidding war. She was lucky.

She doesn't know how lucky. The bike is one-of-a-kind. It has new custom paint, stop sign red, with a yellow and a blue pin stripe on the gas tank and fenders replacing the original two white stripes. Kurt painted the bike himself, meticulously; he never settles for anything less than perfection. Folks who don't know a vintage BMW when they see one mistake it for brand new. It's always kept clean, going to the back yard for a complete wash and de-greasing after every trip. I have a bucket full of brushes, each specially suited to clean wheels or fork boots or another part of the bike's anatomy. It has after-market wheels and seat and other extras that make it more attractive, more dependable, and easier to ride than a stock bike. And despite the ninety or so thousand miles on its odometer, its mechanical condition is as perfect as Kurt could make it. After sitting in the barn for three years, it started up this spring like it had just been ridden yesterday. It's ready to go to the far reaches of the continent and has already toured much of it.

The bike and I traveled to most states and provinces, from the Rio Grande to Northwest Territories, from the Pacific Coast Highway to Daytona, with lots of memories packed into the miles in between. It taught me to love the northern prairies and all the other places I once thought were boring. It hauled me through the most diabolical road construction detours out west, rolling through holes, wobbling over rocks, and slithering along in greasy mud, always carrying me through without mishap. It taught me staying upright is what's important, whether I look good doing it or not. It never let me down, except for the time an after-market clutch failed a hundred miles from home, and once when the battery died in the middle of a bike-packed street during rally week in Sturgis, South Dakota. Easily forgiven lapses, obviously not the bike's fault. When I was out of the country and riding only once or twice a year, it always felt easy and familiar, like we were never apart. It was a trusted friend for eighteen years, though ridden only once in the last five, as I gradually lost the physical capacity to ride.

We don't talk much about why I'm selling the bike. Rosie sees my useless looking left hand, my clutch hand, and offers me a reflexology treatment before she leaves. I politely decline, explaining I have nerve damage.

"I don't know if I'm a red bike person. I was hoping to buy a black one," Rosie confesses.

"It'll grow on you," I assure her. "And what better color for someone named Rosie?" I tell her how I've tried to color coordinate my riding apparel over the years, with red shirts, red-framed sunglasses, and finally, a red jacket to match the bike.

Rosie suits up after finishing her tea, dons a black nylon jacket and full-face helmet, and morphs into just another unisex, anonymous motorcycle nut. She gets on the bike and her legs are as short as I feared when I first saw her. Answering a query about seat height on eBay, I recommended a thirty-two inch inseam for a potential rider to comfortably put both feet flat on the ground. Rosie looks like a twenty-something inseam. But she teeters confidently in her thick-soled boots and rolls out the driveway for a short test ride. She obviously knows what she's doing; we can hear her smooth shifting at just the right acceleration points. She's smiling when she returns, satisfied she can ride the bike home. As she prepares to leave, we wish her well, and for the fourth or fifth time tell her to let us know if she ever has any questions. I climb into my car and drive off, leaving early for a dentist appointment, so I won't see my bright red obsession roll out the driveway for the last time.

I'm depressed for several days. I feel like I did when I asked the vet to put my sweet, old and failing cat to sleep. Kurt doesn't seem to comprehend my feelings at all and has annoyed me through the entire selling process with his endless chatter about it. I've only barely resisted the urge to holler, "Shut the hell up!"

"You sound like you've lost your best friend," observes an understanding colleague on the phone. It's worse than that; I've lost part of my identity. For years, there was never any question about where I'd be on a weekend or vacation day between April and November. I'd be on the bike. Bosses at work teased me about it, amused that the woman in the conservative gray suit had a wild, biker chick alter ego. So now what shall I do? Mourn the loss of "my beautiful wickedness" and melt away like the wicked witch clutching her flying broomstick in the *Wizard of Oz*? No, I'll survive this loss, but I don't want to talk about it.

A couple weeks after the bike's departure, I receive an e-mail from Rosie. Do we know anything about how to lower the bike? Yes, we do, and we send her ideas, along with names and web links for several resources. She admits to having bought a new jacket that's partly red. She asks if the bike has a name. Despite our long friendship, I never thought to give my bike a name. A week or so later, I receive another e-mail. Rosie's purchased a stock seat she hopes will be lower, and she's christened the bike "Glory, Glory." The bike's growing on her. I try not to think about it.

CRAVING

I may have been mistaken to think it was the motorcycle I loved and needed most. The bike is gone and I'm still seduced by diesel fumes, turning to see the name painted on a semi's door announcing where the eighteen-wheeler calls home. Its diesel whine brings to mind nights in cheap motels and campgrounds crammed along the highways. Omnipresent neon glares, road warriors' noxious nightlight. The perfume of Everyman's motel room is a distinctive, yet indescribable potpourri of must and lust, industrial strength cleaner, cigarette smoke, chlorinated linens, anticipation, regret, disappointment, desperation. Sleep can be stingy in such places, another toll a traveler pays to access the commerce and escape routes.

I loved car trips as a child, being transported on Sunday afternoons down country roads that offered trees and lakes, fresh corn, sweet cherries, melons and tomatoes. I roamed those places again in my first car, an ancient, quirky Beetle. My photography class assignments were an excuse to bumble along back roads I didn't know. I wasn't certain what I was after, but was convinced I'd know it when I saw it and it would be photogenic.

I had no bike in Europe, so wandered in my rental car, down winding roads in the Ardennes, across a *dijk* to Friesland, through the harbor maze to Lillo, where sheep grazed unperturbed beside a nuclear power plant. I got lost in Rotterdam, kept going till I reached the ring, a destination where old roads always lead if you have the nerve to persevere. I found my courage and hung on tight, drove while disoriented, on a foreign side of the road in the British Isles. Through roundabouts and narrow streets, Yorkshire Moors and Dales, past castles, pubs, cathedrals, the invisible frontier, the worst snow storm in a quarter-century. I learned why side mirrors fold inward when I dove into a buffering hedge like a startled hare.

It's the getting to somewhere that excites me. I gather and study maps, find the long way around and memorize routes. I love the snowbird's drive to Florida, spending all night on the road nestled in the rocking chair between big rigs on mountains, sliding around the curves in rhythm to whatever's on the radio. Each pit stop is a different climate, warmer, more botanical, with smells of clover, wild onion and swamp, frog and cricket music, day-old Krispy Kremes, a sorghum syrup dialect. Waffle Houses and billboards for mill outlets and tourist trap purveyors of fireworks and pecan logs sprout everywhere like mushrooms that may be safe to eat or not.

Though I prefer meandering down not-always-on-the-map roads, there's magic on the super highways. Once upon their path, there's no need for a map. There's nothing stopping you but the biology of humans and their motor vehicles. Only hours separate you from bougainvillea in October, or mountain snow in July. An experienced time traveler, your mind can touch it all now. Rolling onto the freeway entrance ramp, you're there already in some dimension.

WOMAN MARKING TIME

Karen Marie Duquette

The soothing quality of letting go, when words emerge, is why I write. Mere seconds pass and inklings, just on the brink of knowing, sashay about in my head—teetering things, only passing inclinations, not even clear thoughts I jot down. I'm startled by this part of myself, marking white paper, partaking in the process of writing, owning it.

There is an allowing quality to writing as words fall on the page. I can let go of my past. Enjoy again. Overcome anxiety. Well-used or not, time marks a person.

I can manage the wrinkles and weight of life, go beyond the fear. There are, however, those events we can neither plan nor expect. We can only go on, learn from the knowing that's left in the wake of it all.

And the explosion of joy, always surprising me, like a splintering of green in March's giving way to spring—I can talk about in my way, in my own singular voice.

I can place my mark as the swell of experience rises about me. I can write a thought down. Make a poem. Tell a story. Say something, freefalling without limits. I can write caveman-style if I must. Or sketch what I can't say. But I'm leaving my mark.

Try this:

Obtain a dollar store notebook and collect your thoughts there. Use it as a journal of sorts, recording everything you come across as you read and go about your life—poems, words and images from magazines that jump out at you, a quote from a classical source or a calendar's inspiration you paste in beside your thoughts. Go vivid in color. A collage record of you and your everyday happenings makes fodder. Write from it. An intention taken note of has a better chance, once it's written down. Date your inky thoughts—not in any order. Stay away from linear. Thoughts are chaos. Let yourself go.

Now, you—make a good story!

The Sentinel News   December 31, 2006

PERSONAL AD

Fiftyish female poet, now tuned into writing novels, seeks creative community to nurture her unearthed gift. With a thirst to quench, a cottonmouth come through by way of the mundane. Have you a word? Still with a rotary dial, ring me up.
www.KarenMarieDuquette

POET 1st   in this techno turbo
                   upside-down place
                   where you'll find me.

LIFELINE
A SEA OF WHITE

Through the mist of miserly hanging on

a great white space appeared

empty of lines

unwritten words

urged

OVERCOME BY SILENCE

excerpt from a memoir in progress: Social Security Blues

Knowing I should just cut this man's benefits off and forget about it like everyone else doesn't quiet my thoughts. Within the last hour, I've just gotten off the phone from talking with Mr. Tuttle about his Continuing Disability Review. Twenty minutes I spent on the phone telling him about services available in Michigan's Vocational Rehab or Social Services. Time I didn't have. I couldn't tell him the action I've already taken on his case. He has to wait for his mailed notification. His claim, with his benefits already cut off by an examiner-doctor team in my office, is now before me to make sure the initial cessation of benefits has been made correctly in accordance with Social Security law. Mr. Tuttle's CDR—Reconsideration Claim—left my desk two weeks ago, awaiting a physician's co-signature; now it's lost in the huge backlog of pending cases. My work on his case is done, but procedure prohibits me from telling him. Not that I want to tell him the sad news. Unfortunately, the original decision has been adjudicated correctly, and his twenty years of Social Security Disability payments will end soon, thanks to President Reagan. I have no solutions for him. And I don't have the twenty minutes to talk to him, but I spend the time anyway. As it is, I have to call up a cold bureaucratic affectation in order to terminate the call. I have to get back to the work I can do something about.

Gretchen hurries down the hall in an almost frantic manner, approaching me as I push through the doors separating the administrative offices from the main floor. Something is wrong. That's clear from my co-worker's quick, jerky movements as she picks through cases.

"Gretchen, what's happened?"

The case in my hands is heavy. Clutching it to my chest keeps it up and less of a burden to carry, as I stop to talk with the excited examiner. Gretchen has long, brown hair kept curly around her face—bouncy and tapered down her back. The curls exaggerate her moves, making the words she speaks hard to follow. The hair movement draws me in. I watch the bounce of curls, as they spring around her brown eyes blinking wide open. Hypnotizing, the hair's even placement holds my eyes.

Gretchen sputters, "I'm looking for a case. Some man just shot his head off at the Social Security District Office in Lansing."

"Oh, my God," I gasp. "What's his name?" These words escape as I clutch the case in my hands even tighter, knowing I won't recognize the name, even if it happens to be mine. A backlog of two hundred claims almost never gets to the name recognition stage.

"Tattle, Tuttle, something like that," Gretchen mumbles, starting to move off down the hall to look somewhere else.

"*I've gone as far's I'm going on this.*" Mr. Tuttle's last spoken words circle in my thoughts. The cold response, the one I called up to end the conversation—his last human contact. I don't remember what I said. I just hear how my words sounded.

The walls extend twenty-five feet along a corridor beyond the doors, and there's not another person in the hall. The stillness of the stretch, the isolation of his last speaking reverberates a silent rendering, as a quiet siphoning of air releases words from me, not quite screams.

I just talked to him. My whispered desperation echoes in the hall. The case so heavy seconds before takes flight against the wall—prongs release paper everywhere. Half a yard of papers litter the hall floor, a multi-colored pattern blurring as my memory of that day dwindles to this last act of papers slicing the air.

•   •   •

I have to go back to work. My sick leave has dwindled to less than eight hours. It doesn't occur to me my absence is a result of a work-related incident, and the time lost shouldn't have to be covered by my personal or sick leave benefits. I don't ask for compensated time, and my boss doesn't offer any.

It's hard for me to get up and go. Every fiber aches against the push as I use up my will going to the Disability Determination Service several days after Mr. Tuttle died. Holed up, inside a separate place, half-in and half-out is how I feel. The ripped spaces aren't noticeable. It looks like me walking in the doors of Social Security's Disability Determination Service.

How can one explain snow to a child of the desert? The hollow caress of a haunting cold slaps me when I see a co-worker at the entrance to my workplace. This is the experiencing of a new cold, as if it comes from a desert where snow cold doesn't exist. *Go deeper inside the separate self where snow cold can't be felt,* commands a whisper inside my head. The seductive sounds urge me inside the doors of my employer, beside the co-worker who doesn't want to be near me.

Walking stiff-legged toward my desk, I see groups of people. I can't speak. It's all I can do to walk. They stop talking among themselves as if I might hear them or care about what they are saying. I can't feel the floor beneath my shoes.

More people stop and stare. They don't speak to me as I walk by. All avert their eyes, as if the sight of me is too much of a disturbance. Inside me, I feel the union leader look away first, then the disability examiner. A little girl that's me looks away next. Finally, the woman who begins to shake tries to look away. The seeing of this takes place at a very deep level, by someone else removed from me, recording it as if it's a dream.

The air is so thin, swirling beneath my lips. There isn't enough room in my chest to breathe. I pull my purse up to my chest and hold it there, as if it will help me breathe. The sight of the people I know so well drawing away from me casts a spell. I join the others watching the shaky woman from a distance, as if she's not me. I don't see clearly. Off to the side, a peripheral vision takes over. Straight ahead floats a narrow band of fuzzy, but direct, linear light. I find my desk by following that light.

Seated now, I feel my breathing lighten up a bit. Sights and sounds swim around inside my head, fighting to get my attention. The cases, with mail stuffed in them haphazardly, are piled every which way on the desk. The familiar brings me to a place. I know now where I am. The need to do something without thinking forces me to open a case on top. The phone rings. I look long at the echo of the sound as it rings again. I pick up to quiet its ringing.

"Social Security Disability Determination Service" springs from my lips, a welcome routine replacing the need for me to think.

"Is this Karen Duquette?" the voice inside the phone demands.

A hollow voice answers, "Yes."

"My name is Jessica Castile. I'm with the *Today Show*." She begins the conversation as if this is a normal interchange that happens every day with a disability examiner in Lansing, Michigan. Her manner is businesslike. She is assertive as she speaks.

"We want you on the show next week. We'll give you an all-expense-paid trip to New York, First Class, everything." She stops here, as if her job is done, expecting me to come to New York because she asks and is going to pay me.

"We will have Michigan's Senator Levin and you, the person responsible for stopping Mr. Tuttle's Social Security." She pauses, as if genuinely curious. "Can you tell me why you took his money away, after all these years?"

I feel myself backing my chair away from the desk, as if ready to flee. I am yelling inside my head somewhere, but no sounds come out.

"How'd you get my name?" I whisper.

"Social Security assured me you are the person responsible for Mr. Tuttle's death." From the pounding silence more words emerge, "The Michigan Department of Education confirmed you are the one." She pauses just for a second, as if for effect, and then adds in a polished voice, "I can't reveal my sources, exactly."

The phone call terminates shortly after it began, along with my memory. I can't recall the events happening immediately after, or the things that happened just before, or when exactly this takes place. Karl tells me later he supervised me from 1980 through 1983, when I ask, so my memory's lost somewhere in those years. How the call ends, which one of us hangs up first, remains a mystery to me. What is said in that telephone call might not have been well thought out. The screaming, "Leave me alone!" may not have been spoken out loud.

Thinking of the day I returned to work after Mr. Tuttle died brings me to a silent place. Images come at me. I see a man go to a window where he thinks I am. I see him lift a gun. It's a hunter's gun, but I'm not sure what he actually uses to shoot off his head.

I can't remember particulars. The remembering comes to me at unexpected times. I'm running, and it's all jumbled together when I think. I feel red all around me. A voice or a subtle scene brings me to a place where fear and dread surround me. And I am alone.

I can't tell anyone about it.

SILENCE KILLS

Keeping quiet, not telling blows up your insides,
inflames your sensibilities until there's pain
in every nook and cranny,

a body caving in. Non-spoken smoldering gives
way to the not-so-secret—to others and their
sins infecting your skin, numbing up

an ability to feel. Uncoordinated, discombobulated,
just-off-the-mark movements illustrate
how physically removed you are

from what you once were. Thinking flares in and out.
Vivid haunting stringers of thought flicker about you.
Not-quite-conscious dread hovers

near the point of original harm, where terror eats your
stomach lining, spits your guts out. A phlegm of a life,
lip-syncing to the offbeat, as your body melts,

keeping everything inside; pressure's pent up—
imploding organs disintegrate. The sharp stab
of the previous undoes you.

ON BECOMING

parallel poem based on Elizabeth Spires' poem "Nightgown,"
published in The New Yorker, 9/27/04

To be everyday.
To reside in graceful ease too simple
to be seen distinctly, our intricate odd complications.
To be stacked in symmetry steady and supported,
and then off-balance and slack by design.
To be bent, without a care
and put upon lacking an obvious mark.
Or to hang loose, our willow limbs an arc over wind
knowing full well growth can be torn by a gust into new shadings.

Something great made us.
Something continues to whip us up,
our shape not our own
pulling us this way and that.

Always I look to the moon, attracted to its low hanging,
to its reigning over night an awe-staggering glow.
But I must make do with my little life
in this little time. I can imagine a future,
perhaps already penciled in by a great hand,
where I blur the lines with something of my choosing.

BECOMING FRUIT

I'm his little cumquat,
        he says.
I wonder,
        What does one look like?

My arms and legs
turn into fluid
extensions
of meaty pulp

        succored.

LADYBUGS

are subtle
        like thoughts
you hardly notice

They crawl on outer layers
        dead skin
not flaked off yet

Then wings spread
        off the hard kernel
of an idea

You see possibility
        everywhere
Epidemic the little bugs are

IN PRAISE OF ROOTS

The woods, warmed suddenly by a surprise of April sun lasting several days in a row, surround my dad and me with a crusty smell of earthworm covered by a heady scent of outdoors and its emerald bed of spreading moss. He is at my eye-level, bended knee available for me to lean on, as he pushes leafy green plants aside to look under them, showing me the mushroom, how to pick one so it can grow back next year. I don't want to bother with roots. The woods and plants seem endless, capable of swallowing me up. How can my up-rooting matter?

His arm curves around me as he explains again, him light on his feet and sturdy as the tree next to us, while he tells me how this plant must be left with its base in the ground, so it can grow back next spring. I feel his gentleness beside me. I am the eldest child and the only one big enough to hunt the woods with him. I am filled with the importance of snapping the plant above the ground, and I promise to be careful. I glow where his eyes touch me. I'm old enough to understand, I tell him. I'm six.

Dad's finger on my chin, already yellow from his unfiltered Camels, caresses where my cheeks dimple; then he bops my nose as he sends me in search of edible toadstools. I expect one to jump out of the many layers of jungle hugging my feet. I am sidetracked by white petals with tongues of gold that grow everywhere in these woods. I pick the flowers easier to find, enjoying the fragrance that reminds me of Mother's shower, and I'm glad she's not here to draw Dad away from me. We are alone, just my dad and me in this wonderful woods reeking of spring, mysterious and wet with wonder.

Under the flowers I find one. I can't still my bubbling excitement. The mushroom is in my hands before I know it, its dangling sprouts so easily unearthed.

"Daddy, I'm sorry." I run to him, tears in my eyes, "Can I put the roots back?"

"No, squirt," he says. "You'll have to be more careful next time."

And I manage to be, from then on. From him I learn always to take care with roots and protect them. Once exposed, you can never lay them down again.

POETRY A PLACE
dictionary A-B-C poem

Allay sounds found
in classic poems
abscond A-B-C's ability
to rhyme, a favored absolution ... addle

Brained ... break away
balmy word play
blab balderdash
in borderlands bereft—benigned

Classics and clichés ... calculate
cantos captivating
last century's capricious
capsized cant, cartage of no calm words

Declare deep-rooted deference
doggerel,
don't, do dissonance instead;
dragoon dismantled ditties

Earmarked for executioner, eradicate
express oneself,
emotion, emasculated excrement—
either way, elegance eliminated

Flog fluid words formless,
false face of fanfare
for feigned poetry;
forsake forte—fuck it

Gap grunts goad galleries
graceless grade go-between
groans ... gratuitous graven images
grassroots see a garbled grade of

Hyperbole, do not pay homage
hackles the harbinger of today's
hard tack, haled by it, hamstrung hate
hash, hieroglyphics—half-witted

Ignorant iambic idyll
identified imposters, iconoclast's
inner ear ilk of ill will's impasse,
immortal impact vs inarticulate imagery

Juxtaposed in jut box jumble
jargon's jag jammed in
junior prosody, today's jaded
jousts and jests at his junction

Killjoy or kismet
kindle or kill
keeper or knell
katydid kinfolk to Keats

Love lyrics, lifeblood's luminous words
lucid language lofty, likeable
lament linguists lost loyalty to
Longfellow ... listen to the

Music, maestro's machinations
magic made, metaphor's mainspring
majestic muse, masterpiece malleable
mandates the masses, marriage made of

Napalm's narration, now the novelty
and nemesis of not new poetry,
necromancy naïve looks down her nose
in niche's newfangled nonsense not told

Oblivion of old, overshadowed by
Orpheus outlasted, onerous ouster
orchestrates orders opaque, ought
over awe, off-beat oncoming

Poetry palliates Pandora's purr
pop-in-jay pollutes, purebred
prosody paragon par excellence
poignant prose purloins

Quietude, quintessence queues quest
quite simply quells
quarrelsome's quatrain;
quantum leaps to

Raptures roped raw-boned rampant
realist reading recondite
red herring reflections of
refractory regency

Sublime, shock the stutter
so solitary strolls
soliloquy no more,
step sophisticated

To triumphant talk
trajectory tableau
tragic talebearer tailspins
a tangled take, do tell

Us ubiquitous uncommon man
unify urban utterances
undreamed of, undaunted
unable to unyoke, old-new

Voice is viable
vignette vintage
verb-vowel volleys
voyage of verbiage

Welcome; work-wise ways
wield witticism
witness worlds wide with woe
weak world-class words, woolgathering

X
Yesterdays,
Zero
The Place of Poetry

TENDING
ghazal

Oil skims the surface of water pooling above the firm ground in inky violet
swirls—at odds and beautiful, together yet not mixing.

You, never good-looking, catch his eye. He talks through your can-care-less.
You, always listening. And water runs the surface, a fire flowering desire.

A violent sky, orange and golden, wild with flame, turns pink and blue slivered;
longstanding colors don't bow to each other, then mark a horizon majestic.

The day is ordinary. You open your eyes, touching the man beside you.
Each is a life, an idea expanded. Allow its drifting to mirror and hold.

Bury a seed in shallow dirt, while you worry away weeds. Using a hoe,
your fingers, anything handy to keep up a life; tending the garden is hard work.

HAIKU

After a stone cold
passage without oil's respite
spring leaps—splinters life.

NEVER WANTING

The wrong mood for him to be honing in on me
with his soft fingers rough from his fixing a thing—
unruly after overwork or neglect, unlike me,
never wanting for his attentions—occasionally
like today, could do without a care ... but
instead, his hands are drawn to me and rest
on an imposition, quietly at first, until I don't know
where I begin and he leaves off; our skins intermingle
like hot suede aglow—inside, seedy with musk,
an odor arising rife from an emitting
separate unto itself ... insinuating his want
for mine until the craving takes on a life
beside and among us, swift in an uptake
desirous of more, movement caresses
each to the other, innocent again are we;
our first time over and under and in between
experienced like new, is new—a sigh
escaping.

HIS FIRST LOVING

from a novel in progress: Catrell's Love

Claude notices the thin swamp weed stuck up out of the water. The lone reed stands out like a ghost amid the river's spring-fed gurgling, inviting him to think on Sadie. Her hair's languid waving he remembers. It touched just below her waist twisting ten colors into several shades of yellow and brown, while being neither. The thought of her takes his breath away.

Soon as she could, that girl had been yelping at his heels every time he turned around—Beacher's grandbaby, near half-grown girl. It was her thirteenth year, his fifteenth, he remembers, when he saw her as a woman for the first time.

The smell of her surrounds him. His eye catches her subtle changes, and they're pinned up in his heart and mind, where he savors them to keep them untainted. She looks at him in that *I know what you're thinking* way and shakes her head, baring a long throat, her *kiss-me-here* gently sloping into breasts that weren't there before. When did the woman appear in that girl?

Shirtless, he has his loose knee-pants held up by suspenders sagging in the back where one side's let go, hiding his growing need to touch her. Claude doesn't question his want. Sadie's become a part of him, closer than kin. When had his loving appeared? Near as he can tell it had been gradual. Like the drop of dew meandering down a milkweed's fuzzy leaf, hanging in the fluff, washing its way down into nothing falling to the ground—seductively slow, kind-of-sudden gradual he accepts but can't explain.

"Gotcha." Sadie unfastens the lone strap holding up his britches in the back and then quickly retreats behind the rock-climb out of reach, to watch and be ready to run in case he chas'd after her. Her eyes never leave his.

His suspenders slither up past his neck before he can react. With the thin cloth released, gravity forces his pants to fall wrinkling around his ankles. At the same time, he digs his bare feet into the creek's dirt, taking quick steps to chase after Sadie, and is felled like a tree face down into the river's marsh, twisted up by his pants and turning quickly to catch a hold of this girl-child turned woman.

"Sadie Beacher!"

She laughs. Sadie's delighted-to-be-alive mirth sprinkles around him and his bare-naked soul like magic dust flung by a wood sprite. He feels clean again after the night full of his ma's touching him where a mother shouldn't.

Claude lies perfectly still, his face kept hidden in the weeds, and drinks in her glee, enjoying her happy sounds, her smell—his now camouflaged desire to make love with her is even stronger, pulling at him to reach out to the woman in her, despite her childish, teasing tricks. And he feels love for Sadie. He's sure of it now.

Seconds, hours pass—he's not sure. Claude hears her curious steps moving towards him as she sheds her rock shield. One. Then two. She sneaks inch by inch in the direction of his lying still. He hears her silent questioning, confusion at his play-possum pose apparent in her slow timid steps.

Did I hurt him? He senses her thinking as if she spoke, thoughts jumping between them effortlessly.

Claude smiles as she reaches down to touch his back, jabbing at him as if to wake the fearsome dead, timid then bold with her hand's shaky movements. "I'm not sleepin' Sadie," Claude says.

"Oh." She pauses. "Are you hurtin'?" Sadie lays her hand on his shoulder, lightly caressing, no longer child-like. She slides her fingers to the small of his back and the gentle rising slope of the muscles there.

Claude's voice rumbles in his throat. He grasps her ankle and pulls her down beside him before he turns his head, revealing a burning in his blue-gray eyes. He buries himself in that space between her face and breast, kissing her neck softly, breathing in the newness of touching her as a woman for the first time.

Startled, she calls out, "Claude," as if his name clears her mind and gives him permission to respond. Like a child picking up a toy, she fondles him. He sees her eyes become aware of his love, of her own desire. He feasts on her palomino eyes—a pale and golden smoldering scalds him while she becomes acquainted with the havoc and joy threading through her body. He touches where she quivers.

Sadie explodes, giving voice to what's shaking her through her clothes.

Dedication ~

> *"His First Loving," and the poem to follow, "Narcissus As a Mother," are dedicated to men, the forgotten victims of abuse. For the times before bad men become monsters, almost without exception, they are mom-made.*
>
> *To those grown men who, by force of will, somehow choose not to warp—I applaud you.*

NARCISSIS
AS A MOTHER
ABC darian poem

Above the sounds of cooing
Beneath a baby's being
Coddled by this mother—

Dwells a woman devoid of
Either caring or the ability to love, except
For her alone she stares; always drawn to
Glance toward a mirror reflecting
Herself or her beauty she sees in her son,
        she competes with her daughter

In effect the children are
Just
Kept to channel

Love back toward her, the
Mother; a son is
Not
Offered real warmth but given
Physical motions—not
Quite emotions, simply
Rutting
Sex
This
Udder
Vexing
Woman

X's and O's
Youth sacrificed to her erogenous
Zones, zebra mother, horse of a different color

THE ANIMAL WITHIN US

The animal in us takes over at a certain point
    At a certain point we break

We break and cross over, and the animal takes over
    The animal is always with us

Within us, under all that's human it lies
    Under all that, hewn and battered if broken

If broken, we could do what an animal does
    Could do that, what terror creates it perpetuates

Created and perpetuated, when the animal in us takes over
    When the animal in us loses all the human edges

All the human edges are—but fragile wings
    Fragile wings transform into the animal within us—

        when broken

YESTERDAY'S

supper is lost in the refrigerator's jumble
like an African warrior, recently captured.

Your woolly mammoth of meat
has grown large tusks. Giant dust balls,
like those found in antique stores' retiring corners,

circle what once was. I see foam
come from your mouth; a London fog
issues from what you no longer want.

Rotten egg smells, our chemistry
gone awry has opened Pandora's box.
My softball bat is not soft. The words

winding around the bruise swell,
I love you turns yellow,
I'm sorry hollows a purple center,

crimson echoes, *I'll never hit you again.*
I run.
My windmill

of intent
doesn't catch the wind
of your words.

HER PLACE
WOMAN MARKING TIME

In the beginning every word you utter
sparkles in my ears with private meaning,
and a heartfelt shiver nicks me, a telltale sign—
your brand's already on my spine.

Early on, I fall into you, forgetting myself
in a hurry to be one. It's no wonder a woman
takes on a man's name. We're quartered then
packaged, since Adam, prime cut—part your rib.

Living swells around a seaming in of a woman
into wife, into mother, into whatever—needs
taken care of. We become outside of our self, losing
touch with the woman touching the man touching the woman.

And then, life takes on a certain meaning found only in the being
a twosome. You and I create a space; I no longer am.
Now is the time when my hold on myself loosens and slips
from my sense of knowing me, into a no longer important—me.

The fault is not yours, me you love, love so completely.
I give myself up willingly, no longer aware of where
I am separate, or what is important to the she imbedded in the he,
letting loose of woman's hand, to take hold of a man's—instead.

Midlife and split, unbeknownst to her, woman carries on—
unperturbed by the dull ache seeping around inside her female life
of cycle's ebb and flow, she troubles unique, that carry-all labeling
when a man can't put a finger on what is bothering his other half.

What is it? Eyes soft amid laugh lines, there's at times a frown—a life
leaving behind parts of herself in others; a son, and a great love for her man
leads back around to the well-used, time-marked woman. Awake in the now.
She's still there, honed, and ready. Time, yet, to make of it what she can.

The gradual re-acquaintance, Old Man Time falling away, leaves her open to think first of herself, to look for her place. She finds the thread of solitary self, notched and pointing, to where she's been all along; dimly her shadow stands up—a silhouette cast on long forgotten stone, foundation's wall, still a cave after all this time.

A VIEW OF SUTTONS BAY

Protecting the space
        water galleys
beyond the window

Autumn leaves tumble
        freefall
has rescued their brown hanging

Purple sky
        layered
pink and blue sliced with white

Green still
        populates
the distant shore, houses ever hidden

Bare limbs
        sweep forward,
presenting the bay

A wash in wonder
        calm today,
silence kinder than human noise

DANCING IN TIME

Mary Simion

Writing is now my dance, though it wasn't always. As a teen and through my twenties, I loved dancing, especially the jitterbug, with my friends to the music of the big bands of the day in ballrooms in and around Detroit. I have incorporated this activity into my poetry as a metaphor for my life and a touchstone of recollection, a technique I have often used when wondering what to write about and how to get started.

After many years of not trying to write, I was inspired by the first Middle East war, Desert Storm. I felt compelled to say something about the women in combat, which was something previously unacceptable in our culture. I wrote a poem about such a soldier. As I began writing, the images grew strong in my consciousness. After that, my creative mind and imagination went into gear, and I began seriously writing. My husband was himself inspired and joined me in workshops and creative writing classes. We learned to plumb the depths of our lives and experiences, express our feelings in simile and metaphor, and begin writing our memoirs as creative nonfiction and poems.

We began simply, finding themes in nature and in our everyday lives, our pets, the weather, fishing, work, our parents' attitudes and struggles, our mothers' cooking, our stages of growing up, our children, especially the recent death of our son, even each other. This you can do! Let your creative mind freefall. Also read as much as you can of fiction and nonfiction. Read a poem a day.

I strongly urge everyone to look into the mirror of time, peer into past areas of life and tell about it. Write it down, even if it seems awkward at first.

If you need help, try to find a writing group, workshop or class. There are even classes on-line. Local groups are often mentioned in the newspaper and are usually minimal in cost or free. You may find many new friends with similar interests in writing who started out on your very same footing. Good luck to you! I'm still freefalling and dancing on this great stage through life.

 Try this:

You might begin by remembering a teenage activity, like dancing or some other hobby or sport that you enjoyed in youth. Write down what you can remember or tape record yourself telling the story of a particular incident that seems important or brings up strong emotions. Try writing it as if in a diary, and then expand and try to make a story of it, perhaps not even about yourself. Invent a character. It's easier to write about someone else, as you don't have feelings of guilt or self-consciousness. Then, if later you want to make that person you instead of the hero of a story, you can convert it. As you read poetry or prose, try writing in the style of the author, using your own words but following the author's pattern. Surprise yourself with the art that comes from your effort.

DANCING IN TIME

It don't mean a thing if it ain't got that swing.
~Duke Ellington

I spoke to them in tongues of time,
danced my frenetic jitterbug
to *White Heat, String of Pearls,* Artie, Glenn,
Frank, Big Bands, top brass in white jackets,
but then you, baby, spoke to me
in the loud voice of rock-'n'-roll,

perpetual beat of rock-'n'-roll.
You said it was now *your* time.
In your high voice you spoke to me,
as the world shrugged off jitterbugs,
flicked off Artie, Frank (gone cats); their jackets
hung on empty, while the Atlantic swallowed Glenn.

Tears fell like pearls on the floor for Glenn,
picked up to the rhythm of rock-'n'-roll.
Big Bands, double bass, brass, white jackets,
all wrapped in time, our time, war time.
Frenesi, A-Train, Brown Jug, Jitterbug,
and you sang of the Beatles to me?

It was like *Middle C* to me.
Tears fell on ballroom floors for Glenn,
as Artie, Benny, Frank and we jitterbugs
sank in the seas of rock-'n'-roll.
You talked to me in cruel tongues of time.
Then Frank took off his old, white jacket.

The brass trombone, clarinet, their jackets,
heavier than electric guitars to me,
the highs, lows, notes of my time,
like tears, fell on my thoughts of Glenn,
dead of war and Woodstock, rock-'n'-roll
with Artie, Benny and us jitterbugs.

By the bandstand in the park among litterbugs,
I smile at the thought of the bands' white jackets
in the Levi's world of rock-'n'-roll.
It's a ludicrous comparison to me
of *Black Dog* to *In the Mood*.
I blow a few raspberries from my tongue of time.

Frank crooned through our jitterbug crack in time.
We cried when Glenn died in his major's jacket.
Rock-'n'-roll never meant a thing to me.

6 JUNE 1944

on receiving a Limpet's shell said to be from Normandy

From what Atlantis came
this lifeless ocean bone,
a footed limpet's hide,
cast by wave or dropped by lunar tide
upon a relic-scattered beach
where muscles of another order
set their combat-booted spinning
feet to fight upon that ancient
Celtic cliff-protected shore?
Swept by artillery, repelled by Stygian storm,
Achaean-like through mounting fire,
grenade and heavy rifle laden, they
climbed on knotted ropes and ladders
to a higher plane or fell and died
on sand that shows no scar.

Six-thousand-three were hit by mortar shells.
Those casting mortal shells aside,
like the limpets, rose to light.

CURTAINS

Fish swim on my window blinds,
yellow perch, salmon, rainbow trout.
The shades remind me of my son,
dying in deep sleep, his heart caught
in a net of dreams, snagged, stopped
like the wind-up watch he wore
when he went fishing as a boy.
Fish obey the sun and moon, not
chronology imposed by springs.

They say that night is darkest
before first light and fishing
best as red dawn's fingers lift
that veil so fishermen can see
to bait their hooks, especially
in September, month of scales and
equilibrium. Before sunrise
my first born goes to where
the biggest fish are sure to bite.

He stands, his vessel rocks.
He lifts his arm to cast for bass
or walleye, gets a string of perch
or northern pike, perhaps within
the river's mouth, happy in his little boat.
The outboard throbs through morning mist
across a white-capped channel.
He docks upon the other shore.

Beside my windows I release
the folded shades to free the fish
he ventured last to find and catch,
the fish no one on earth can match.

FROM THE GARDENS OF NEPTUNE

Arms strong, headlong, my son the diver
swims beneath a violet veil of waves,
glides deep along the steep geanticline,
down through a forest thick with kelp,
to find the arch of Neptune's silent garden
where, from slimy weed-wound rocks
he frees the tasty foot
of Haliotis Rufescens, prized red abalone.

He discounts the hunger of the sharks,
Great Whites and Hammerheads,
patrolling in these waters and known
to guard the garden's gate.
They're drawn to blood.
He takes a chance.

My diver carries Rufescens to shore,
pops him open, peels him with his blade.
The meat removed, the shell reveals
an image of a lost Devonian past,
hidden hereto underfoot,
an imprint of a floating swan to be,
or in another light, a swimming
long-necked reptile like Loch Ness' shown
in opalescent fine, with pearly futuristic
calligraphy of feathers yet to come.

NIGHTSKIES

Night sky covers the vineyard,
a dark globe lighted by strings
of planets, stars, asteroids and out-of-sight
comets, yellow dwarfs, quarks, litter.
My younger son, wrapped in his sorrows,
points like a new Galileo to constellations,
Casseopia, Ursa Major, Gemini,
bright Venus, almost tangibly visible.

I stand here, on the rocky west
edges of turbulent uplift and geanticline,
my eyes searching the sky, head in clouds
mindful of Canis Major's minor howl.

Back home at the lake, the sky by night
hides behind a drape of light
blotting out stars. Machina Electrica, an
astronomical invention, fell by discard
to our planet, a veil between Earth and starlight
though when the Moon is pregnant she can penetrate the pall.

But here, on the edge, the coast is clear,
and there is clarity of firmament.
The sky glitters and twinkles as my
daughter approaches through the vines.
I want to say I see her as a shining star,
You are my lucky star, I shall say. Her eyes will twinkle.
As a baby you were my sunshine; I loved
to rock you in the old moon rocker and sing to you.

There are stars in the sea swimming like fish.
Even the dead swim back in dreams, starring in nightly
performances. Though dead, they return as stars
in oceans of memories. Our star, the Sun, stirs life.
The Moon opens curtains to our stages of the past.

As an infant you lived in an old house.
I was an infant mother with a little son
and a little daughter. We took walks
in the park. You rode in a carriage;
your brother, only three, ran ahead.
As even the dead have windows
to see through, I know he has
run ahead to watch us, looking
through his window in the stars.

GONE FISHING

I don't want to think about
my firstborn dying in his sleep,
his blue eyes closed forever.

To me, he's gone to fish for trout
while I stay home and wait to hear
on his return from distant streams,
how many browns or rainbows
he has or could have caught.

Last time, he took our cat along,
Boomer, centenarian, ardent
fisher in his youth but fast
foundering in age and fishing dreams.

The catch, this time, the sad catch
was—neither one came back.
No smile, no kiss, no fish, no purr.

POEM OF LIFE

From ancient earth I came to live my poem;
the muse came up from antique tracts
that set me down in time to strains of life,
and I am here to live my poem as fact.

Primordial myth from dark and bloody ground
gave me metaphors, and sprites
like spirits of all starry nights
stirred my genesis and genes in time
to rhyme and take a path my spirit shows to me.

My father's itchy foot, my mother's river caves
prepared a place where I could grow
propelled by Aries' and far-sighted father's fires
below rock cliffs of Capricorn, a climbing goat;

within deep chthonic pools
swam my little fishes, schooled in Braille
to many stranger sites with reeds entwined
in shallow, like Sargossan seas.

My spirit sang in youth, still sings as voice
grows cracked with over-use and age
though music of the spheres resounds.
I sing an *A*, Spirit whispers *out of tune,*
give me a scale, a chord for Pisces' zither.
Close harmony of gods is all around.

I fear no ghost, no ogre from the accidental dark
or blood upon the door I do not force.
From ancient muddy myth, from Jupiter and Mars,
Sun, Moon, Neptune and now, *Niobe, comes the poem
that I live in, the poem swims through to me from all eternity.

"Mind now! Mind me!" my mother mentor says.
"Give it no never mind," my father's voice insists.
"Just use your head, follow your wish and dream."

Through mazes of ascendancy from ape to relativity,
from fire to flight from Earth to rise from mud again,
to live the poem, the metaphor, the myth.

*Niobe was so proud of her children they were taken away.

AU SABLE HOLY WATER 1959

At dawn the first morning
we awaken in ferns.
Our eyes hold the glimmer
of yesterday's water.
Two golden eagles survey
our bivouac from their lookout
on top of a tall white pine.

We put in late, too late to make camp,
in clouds of mosquitoes and air raids by gnats.
Tents still in the ribs of our Old Town canoe,
we unroll our beds on the fern-furled bank
of the white-crested, fast-running stream.

We lay down on fronds, our primeval pallets
and wake to the buzz of black flies.
His pole hooked and baited, our son runs to fish,
our daughter combs out her long hair.

We fry trout for breakfast, bury the bones,
smother and drench our embers.
On our knees at the river, we wash up our pans
and take pictures to help us remember.
We pack up our gear and put out again.

Silently dipping, gray water rippling,
like thunder rumbling clear through the channel,
when the sun sets we will put in again
and peacefully sleep in the ferns.

WOLF AT THE WINDOW

Once, I lived another life in a much older house in Royal Oak, two blocks east of Woodward Avenue. I had only two children, a little boy, Tommy, who at five had just started kindergarten, and a little girl, Ruthie, not quite three years old. In fact, you may remember the story of how one morning in April we discovered fairies dancing in the back garden. We knew they were really there because we all three saw them leaping about in the dew. Those were the days when the fabulous and metaphorical wolf was often at the door, and when we felt ourselves fortunate to have a house and door at all. At that time, too, we lived under the aegis of Tom's Market's blinking sign which flashed its high, bright, red neon on our front bedroom windows. TOM'S TOM'S TOM' (the final "s" was out, which was also annoying). All of this flashing came all the way from Woodward two blocks over intervening roofs all night long. Of course, we pulled the shade, but it proved to be too transparent, and we were still disturbed at maximum tolerance (or intolerance) by its aggressive, penetrating, pulsing thrusts into our most private quarters—our bedroom. It was a sign to be noticed and impossible to ignore. The only way it could be even half-diminished was by opening our adjacent closet door as wide as possible, so that half the flash was blotted out—but half was still boldly visible. M'S M'S M'. After long suffering this offensive and invasive display, we complained, first to the market where we traded our paycheck for food. They were unable, they said, to do anything about it. They had no control. Their suggestion was to *put heavier drapes at the windows.* Well, heavy drapes in the winter was one thing, but in the heat of summer, they added unwanted warmth and a stuffy atmosphere to a small room.

We next approached city officialdom. What you read in the papers today of the fate of complaining citizens anywhere when they go hat in hand to the elected political hierarchy, you should know that things were no different then. The response is at first almost always negative to taxpayers who ask for anything, whether for signage changes or extermination of rats in the alley. They said there was nothing they could do, try Venetian blinds, first find blinds to fit and then install the hardware. They were not as heavy as the drapes but did not work as well. We could still see the red flashing TOM'S TOM'S TOM' through the louvers. Our nightlife seemed permanently lit up. We finally added an overlay of white drapes to the Venetian blinds. None of this was without traumatic consequence. The worst and most worrisome was the effect on our little son, Tommy, who began to take exception to our negative attitude toward the flashing sign. He began, we thought, to take it personally, now that he was printing his first name and last initial in bold letters on his school drawings. TOM S TOM S TOM S.

Our little daughter, Ruthie, not quite three, could not yet read but did respond to colors. One night I tucked her into bed in her front bedroom next to mine. As usual, I read to her and sang a song or two as I held her on my lap in the rocking chair. Soon afterward, I heard the sound of crying coming from her room. I rushed in to see what was the matter.

"Mama!" she cried. "There's a pink wolf trying to get in my window."

I went to the window. "I don't see a wolf. It must have gone home. Just close your eyes and go to sleep."

"No! No! Don't leave me!" This was serious.

I carried Ruthie to the rocking chair. "I'll sing you some songs," I said and launched into *Rock-a-bye Baby* and a verse from Brahms' *Lullaby.*

"I see it!" she screamed. "It's trying to get in the window!"

"I'll look," I said and went to the front window. Then it dawned on me. It wasn't a wolf or even an apparition. It wasn't a nightmare. It was a much flashier intruder—the red Tom's Market sign. Another drape-hanging was in order.

FATHER

sonnet

Our father is the measure of all men,
the one we want to please, to prove our worth.
He, who is our guardian and gauge,
ruler, until coming of our age,
who, in our urgent struggle to be free
we sometimes rage, rebel against and say,
We'll show you what we're made of! and it's *he.*
Our father points the paths to our escape.

He is our conscience, angel in disguise.
Lost in our youth, we have lost our guide.
Our later loss may well renew the chain
to child we were—to child within.
For long before our father's work is done,
he wills to us the ways to walk alone.

ON VAN GOGH'S STILL LIFE *IRIS*

In March just shy of vernal equinox
light snow falls while I await green pips
of iris leaving through spring breaks in icy beds,
breaking out of winter prisons in uprise,
a riot of fast budding stems.
I look for stakes.

I place my stakes to give support
to their brief hegemony, to hold their heads.
My irises, a long-lost neighbor's gift,
short-lived Dutchmen, three days' bloom
then the withers, blossoms droop,
putrid on still living stalks.

My father called them *flags*
because of wave and early fail,
their brave display pre-empted
by final seep and withering,
a rancid ooze remains,

To see the constant glory
of *Iris* by van Gogh,
bearded though they be,
caught forever in their prime,
is to see ephemera quite trapped
in time, in blink of eye.
Live irises show fears of dying soon,
by dropping morbid tears so near the start.
Three days from bud to bloom to blasted age
they must return to prisons of rhizomes.

Gardeners know the floral life unstill,
the moving *other* sides of art.

THE OPEN WINDOW
… remembering the victims of Hurricane Katrina,
whose pain blew 'round the world

As Mamá and I left our drowning house, we climbed down an old trumpet
vine. We lingered far too long as waters rose. I tried to close the window left
behind. A boat full of strangers stopped to save us from the flood, but the
open window stuck in Mamá's mind. Deciding then to stay or go seemed
more than she could manage. As the leaking levee finally dissolved, Mamá,
too, dissolved in tears, declaring, should she have to leave, she'd die. If she
had to leave her house, her treasured things, why go on living? She knew she
had to go, but in her mind there was more concern for things than fear for
life.

People in the boat shouted, *Please, Ma'am, try to hurry! The river's rising now
right smart!* as they struggled with the swinging trumpet vine. Orange
blossoms launched like a toy flotilla, a trumpet flower speedboat race
downstream.

I felt foolish saying, *I must close my window,* as I clambered down the vine I
feared would break. While Mamá hollered, *Don't leave that window open!* But
I couldn't get a grip, and I couldn't close the window as I climbed.

All the while her temper seethed and wrath rose up. She was loathe to leave
an open window to the world. The people in the boat declared they
understood, but hurricanes don't happen every day. The window, closed or
open wouldn't matter. We must get out and get to higher ground. They said
they understood why Mamá fretted, windows let in rain and thieves, and
snakes are never wanted in the house—never mind the Mississippi River.
They heard her question, *Stay and die or leave and lose my stuff?* Even they as
rescuers could see it was wide open. But I couldn't close the window as I
climbed.

IT SHOULD HAVE BEEN PETER

telling how bad it is, broadcasting the news,
as the wind-driven gulf engulfs our *Big Easy*
city of Jazz and Mardi Gras. Now the band
lays down its cornets and saxes, stills its drums
to watch the levees let the waters in.
The growing flood is chin deep,
right up to the stiff upper lips
and like to lift the roofs of last resort
where victims go to pray for mercy.
They call and wave, hoping for help
in their helplessness. It isn't Peter, it isn't Paul,
it's only Michael, rowing, rowing,
slowly rowing an air mattress downstream,
taking no passengers. Truth to tell
it should have been Peter.

for Peter Jennings, 1938-2005

MY DAY
in memory of Eleanor Roosevelt's newspaper column

It is a day in October, dark and dank,
a day saying rains are on the way,
begun with a mourning of falling leaves,
a day to avoid by staying inside

and trying to think of something
to say or write or do besides raking leaves
and thinking of fairy rings in the grass.
I can open a blank page in my mind

and sit with my wandering thoughts,
scribble my notes, forgetting weather
or not, it doesn't matter,
work on the dishes, laundry, quandaries,

wishes or footwork, body work, handwork,
fill my mental *tabulae rasae*,
as John Locke suggested or might have
suggested had he thought of it

when his October skies darkened
and slunk overhead, slipping
ominously toward winter,
and his property threatened to flood

from the uncontrolled Thames
that no one in their right mind
would have swum in had they known
more about cause and effect.

It is better to read or write
on days like this one than rake
the lawn while leaves hang
by thin fraying petioles, then drop.

I wonder how deep the leaf cover
was in 1610, how it conformed
to the vast forested hills and valleys,
how long it took to compost

and make the bed for the next
generation of land-loving trees
unlocking a new world,
locking the old one out?

"You're out! Locked out!"
we say to you old oaks
and elders, old hickories.
"You have no place to stay!"

LIVE IMAGES

I want a live image taken of my heart
to see if there are still pictures
of my dear ones who have left
the planet for other higher planes.

Is there a mock-up of my mother?
Does she appear as young?
In youth she was so spirited,
determined to succeed, all
with a sense of gaiety and fun.

She went by many names,
Abna, Abny, Elizabeth, Betty,
Daisy, Day, Mama, Mom, Mother.
She called her mother, *Mammy,*
but that was not for her.

Her hair was dark, hung long in waves
and then cut short, though never grayed.
Her smile was warm, her frown could chill.
My mother died still in her prime.

Can you see my dad, depicted
as he was in youth? A quiet
studious boy, thin, slight,
who just when you might think
he was a bore would play
the fool or more outrageous
yet, play you for one and get
a loud laugh from his crowd.

By twelve he held two jobs,
one as stable boy and groom,
the other as a newsboy
delivering the *Courier*
all around the square
in Bowling Green, into

the whorehouse, too.
In the stable he got kicked.
It broke three ribs. About
the whorehouse he got ribbed.

Is my Aunt Annie in the picture
of my heart? She was my refuge,
one who gave me love without a doubt
and never criticized. She had
no other child but me to call her own.
She took me to the picture shows,
to the North Pole at J.L. Hudson's store.
My father's older sister, she died
at ninety shortly after his demise.
She was like another, kinder mother.

Do you see my dear Aunt Nell, the one
whose son was killed at twenty, Little
Kemp, her only child? Her heart then
broke and failed at fifty-five. She was
a gentle genteel woman who strung beads.
She gave to me my fifth great grandma's
china teapot, standing now on my buffet.
She was my father's youngest sister.

Aunt Edwin I felt further from.
She lived way down in Erin, Tennessee.
She was my father's older sister, too,
but seemed more distant to me.
She made hats and strawberry fool.
She had three children, Margaret, Billy, Shirley
Ann. She was the wife of a railroad man
and died the same year as my mother, 1968,
her brain addled by the hats, my father said.
At the end she played with dolls.

Will I see Aunt Winnie in the framework of my heart?
She was my father's oldest sister.
Her indentured smile, her face Lincolnian,
bony cheeks, long nose, chiseled, jutting chin

seemed carved from mountain stone.
She wore the mask of pioneers come round
the mountains, down the rivers, settling in.
Tall and thin, she became the mother when the mother died.

Six were still at home; three soon died as typhoid swept the valley.
Margaret, Tide and Dixie were laid beneath the bluegrass still in bud.
Winnie tied the apron on and set to work.
Typhoid did not touch the rest. She thanked the Baptist God.

At forty-two she married farmer John,
but when he died she couldn't live alone
although she tried to make it on her own.
She moved into a boarding house in town,
the roomers, like a family of friends.
She needed friends when cancer came to stay.

Aunt Winnie died within three days of Little Kemp.
I was fifteen, and I was there to help her to some water.
Morphine caused a thirst.
I sat with her and watched them close her eyes.

O can you see in MRI my Uncle John?
Daddy of my cousins, Cyril, Ben and Ruth
and little John who died when we were six ...
my mother's and Aunt Hollia's younger brother,
husband to Aunt Ethel of the long dark hair,
who let me play on her piano when I couldn't play.
He was a singer, farmer, a kind uncle, a good son
who lost his way and spirit when his soul-mate died.
He died by his own gun at Christmas time
and followed his love, Ethel, to eternity
where they are surely singing side by side
in close harmony praises to the glory of the Lord.

And how about Aunt Hollia, who sniffed snuff?
Short and stout as a teakettle. Her life was tough,
but full of craft and cornbread, biscuits, ham,
fried pies, gravy everyday. And O preserves!
She was a loving aunt who let a one-legged

chicken in the house, so I would have a pet.
Her handmade quilts are my Kentucky cover.
Sometimes, like her, I spout short poems of rage.

Grandmaw and my grandpaw were a pair.
I loved to visit there when I was young.
They had a handmade house,
Four rooms in all and fireplace
big enough to walk in. There were gardens, roses,
and a field of corn, a smokehouse and a well.
The root cellar was cool, dark and had a snake.
Chickens ran around the yard.
Grandmaw was crippled by a stroke,
but she maneuvered with a crutch.
Grandpaw tended everything, gardens,
chickens and to her. He cracked black
walnuts for me on the hearth.
There were no electric lights, no screens.
We went to bed at dark or lit a lamp to see.
Chiggers bit me on the legs. I took a bath in
a tin tub of rainwater heated on the stove.

When they died they were buried on a hill,
side by side. One time Cyril took me to the graves.
He planted flowers there but nothing seemed to grow.

My cousin, Cyril, second child
of Aunt Ethel and my Uncle John,
has been gone now twenty years or more.
He was my friend from childhood days.
He taught me how to milk a cow,
how to get up on a horse and take the reins.
He was like my older brother, on whom I so relied.
When he died, I lost what cannot be regained.
He let me tag along when he went fishing
and helped me look for gold in banks of sand.
He took me down the river in a rowboat
and through the locks with warnings
not to stand. In hard times of Depression
he stayed with us awhile. We went to school

together, hand in hand. He read me funny papers,
Fu Man Chu and *Tarzan* and taught me how to pray,
saying, *Listen, Mary Frances, say Our Father, who art in Heaven …*

Do you see a picture of my son, so young to die,
a fisherman and father, only fifty-nine?
A practicing Boy Scout, in the best of that tradition,
with open mind and gentle heart, goodness
graced his life while he was here.

Are there dogs and cats within the image
of my heart? Do they speak?
Do my dogs wag their tails and lick my feet,
my cats sit upon my lap and purr?
My heart has animals—two Skippy's,
several Blackies, one Boucher, Thor, Hilda,
Mama Cat and her son, Boomer. Poochie, Oyster,
Honey were her darling daughters.
Boomer and my son, Tom, died the same day,
September 17, 2002.
I have a lot of pictures in my heart,
negatives that I would like developed
into live images again, or placed within
a folio of fame, with all their names.

SOLFEGGIO

Don't expect anything and you'll never be
disappointed, my father advised.
What you get is what you get. Be satisfied.
Don't count on others for your happiness.
Your dreams will not necessarily come true.

Mother said to be a Doer, not a Dreamer.
Do not waste time dreaming. Do not
write sad poems and sing sad songs.
Chopin's music is too melancholy.
A dream is not reality. Dreams will make
you sad when they die or are killed.

But Earth was given to me in a dream—
a dream of love and romance my folks evoked.
I, fruit of their pear tree, came from hope.
I woke to find my mind bound in metaphor,
my cortex caught in solfeggio. The intervals
entwined my heart in rhythm, my voice
in syllables, my ears and eyes in rhyme.

Within my dream I dreamed, hoarding dreams,
and thought as others did, acted as expected
and accepted what looked and sounded good,
felt good, seldom looking under surfaces for flaws.

Still, flaws existed anyway and fronts
were often false. The lady upstairs,
with the enticing piano, laughed when I played,
even though she invited me, her four-year-old
neighbor, to try the keys. The piano was out
of tune. I didn't want to play it.
I recognized the hammering of discord.

Nothing could be done right ever again.
The dream turned on its side and into a nightmare
making it impossible to sleep through life,
even though it seemed the only way
without great pain, sorrow and public humiliation.

LOOKING BACK

That it will never come again is what makes life so sweet.
~Emily Dickinson

Lori Goff

Looking back, I find the lure of the open road a creative avenue for me. There's something about the endless passing trees and fields that captures my imagination. A ray of sunshine warming the ground in a dense dark clump of pine trees and a lone, tumbled-down farmhouse beg me to capture their essence in prose or poetry. I always travel with my journal and record those moments of inspiration. Most of the time, I'm a rider enjoying the ride, so I'm free to write and let my mind wander—finding a connection with nature through words.

My writings are a collage of poetry and prose written in sundry forms. I'm inspired by love, family, water, nature, magic. When something triggers my imagination, I'm in a hurry to capture words on paper before I lose them. My thoughts dodge and collide while I search for the perfect image and sound I want to create. Whether I write prose or poetry, long or short, fiction or creative nonfiction, it is the soul behind the words I want to shape and mold.

Poetry has many forms. *Highway Cross* is a concrete poem. It's a combination of the written word and visual art. The content of the poem relates to the created picture. A lone cross on a busy highway hillside inspired me to try this unique form. The setting conjured up many different thoughts and emotions. It's important to me to note the feelings and images I experience when I encounter a moment that evokes a creative response. I jot down phrases and words in my journal, highlighting my personal reactions to the scene. The picture stays with me until I'm able to bring it to paper in poetic form.

Try this:

I began *Highway Cross* by writing three columns of descriptive words, and below these columns I noted related phrases. The center column, being the longer post, required more ideas, and the two shorter columns required fewer words. Then I formatted the words in the cross shape, using a two-line sentence for the arms and one to two words for the center post. What favorite subject from your life would you like to describe in a concrete poem? What descriptive words or phrases would you use? For example, could you write about a hero in the form of a loving heart?

MOUNTAIN WOMAN*

Ain't. Hit. Them.
School on the river
when work called.
No more books for mountain woman.

Met a dreamer.
Rode the ridge
guarded by Granny.
Love decided the fate of mountain woman.

A dozen blossomed.
Stair-step children
filled a log cabin.
Fierce love showered by mountain woman.

Tote the water.
Pound those clothes,
Hang 'em high on the line.
Blown by the wind behind mountain woman.

Back-breaking hoe.
Store supplies
for winter's long.
Eating's longer when tendered by mountain woman.

Pained days.
Gnarled fingers and
chrome knees.
Bent back weighs heavy on mountain woman.

Dreams gone.
Reality wins with
her hard life.
Burdened work the way of mountain woman.

"Mountain Woman," "Death In The Hills," "Healing Touches," and "Granny's Prayer," excerpts from a larger piece.

HEALING TOUCHES

Every hair on my body stands up as I feel the Presence at the foot of my bed. A prickly feeling slowly crawls up me from my toes through the roots of hair on my head. It's a gray feathery form like the hoot owl of the night glowing with a million little yellow-white lights. My throat feels closed, choking off my voice. I can't scream. I can't whisper. My legs and arms don't work. I can't move. Granny, help me, please help me. Oh Lord, I'm so sorry if I'm bad.

"She's aburnin' up with fever. What in the world she been into? Did she go in the creek when I done tole her not to? It ain't summertime. That water's ice cold," Granny asks.

She hears me. Her hand feels so cool on my face and I feel a weight lift off me. The thing is gone but I'm too weak to tell her. I can't open my eyes just yet.

"Get my mustard powder in the black tin box. It's atop the cupboard. I need to make a poultice. It's pneumonie," she cries.

I hear her mixing the powder with water and the spoon hitting her old crock bowl like a whirlybird. When she's satisfied it's smooth as paste, like she done showed me before, she spoons it onto clean white linen. I feel the coolness from the wetness of the cloth, and before long warmth starts to seep into my chest. Someone has piled lots of quilts over me, and I'm hot and cold at the same time.

Granny's pulling the cork out of a brown jug of corn whiskey she grabbed from behind the cupboard. I know 'cause I hear the cork pop and the jug scrape across the floor. The splashing sound of her pouring a shot into a mug tells me she's fixing me a cough remedy. I know she'll add honey and smashed lemon drops, while stirring all the time until the candy melts.

"Maggie, Maggie, cain't you hear me? It's Granny here at your side and your Mama acryin' on the other. Little girl, sip this for me. It'll make you better," she orders.

It's burning, strong-like, but I get it down. Then a spreading warm feeling seems to be working its way down my throat into my belly. Oh, no, I hope it's not that Althea blowing in my mouth. Can't be. Granny didn't say I had the thrush. They say Althea can cure babies with thrush by blowing in their mouths 'cause she don't know who her daddy is. I know Granny won't let her near me. What's the matter with me? I'm seeing things and thinking bad thoughts.

"It's okay, Maggie. We're awatchin' over you. Don't be ascared. When mornin' comes you'll be right here with them that loves you," Granny croons.

My eyes are so heavy. I feel the morning sun coming through the windowpane and warming my face. I open them ever so slowly to see Granny and Mama watching me with tired faces. I lift my hands up and wiggle my toes. Everything seems to be all right.

    "Granny I saw the light and I was afraid. Did you hear me calling you?"

    "I did, Maggie. God wasn't ready to call you up. 'Member what I tole you. He knows ever' hair on your head. He was awatchin' over you."

DEATH IN THE HILLS

"Hear that noise, missy? It's her soul apackin' up and gettin' ready to join her Maker." Granny leans down to whisper in my ear, "Soon there'll be no more sufferin' for her."

Nodding my head, I watch silently as she gently wipes the face of her old friend, Agnes. The gurgling goes on and on as Agnes struggles for air, sounding like the bubbling spring down the hill. Only this sound's a weary heaviness growing louder as she throws her silver head back and claws the air with work-worn hands, as if grasping for peace. Going back to my secret place I think of my baby sister's gurgling, a happy sound I wish for here.

"It's the death rattle and there's nothin' more we do will help her." Patting my thumping chest and kissing my forehead, she straightens up, squaring her shoulders. She takes my hand and I feel comfort from her rough calluses rubbing my palm. Together we turn to find we're facing the family, all of them crying into their red, cracked hands and flowery feedsack aprons.

Granny's shaking head nodding from side to side sends the wailing into loud shrieking screams as she says, "I'm mighty sorry. The high fever and the drownin' water in her lungs is too much for the likes of me to help. It's in God's hands now. We'll be back tomorrow to help dress her for the layin' out."

I steal a glance at Granny as we're walking down the hill. I think I see a tear clinging to her cheek, but she doesn't try to rub it away. She's been telling me all about herbs and remedies for a long time. Now she takes me with her when other folks call for help. I've never seen a tear before and it scares me. "Granny, you'll not ever go and die on me will you? 'Cause I don't want you to."

"Lawdy, Lawdy, child you're adyin' from the moment you're born. No one gets out of this ole world alive. You just 'member I was the one helped born you, and from your first breath I knowed you was special. I chose you to follow my steps, and I'm tellin' you all my secrets, so is you can help others. My time will come, but always know I'm with you. When you hear the gray whippoorwill's call, I'll be up there with him watchin' over you. And when you feel the wet dew on your bare feet, it'll be my tears keepin' you from harm. Now let's not dwell on what will be. For the day's awindin' down and we've got smoked ham to cook for that poor grievin' family."

"It's too late to help Agnes, for they waited too long 'fore sendin' word they needed the likes of me." Granny grabbed my shoulders hard, "I've warned you 'bout pickin' berries with no foot coverin's on 'xactly why Agnes got bit by that copperhead." Granny sighs, "They should have poured sweet milk on the fang holes first thing. Why when Joe Hawks got bit, we wrung the neck on a chicken and slit its breast wide open and plopped it on the bite. One athose ways might have saved her. The poison's spread through her body now."

The next morning, hand-in-hand, the ham tucked in her hickory basket, we go back up the hill and into the dark house that smells of death. Mixtures of sweet and sour vapors hang in the air. The family greets her with warm hugs and sighs of relief. I feel the light touch of pats on my plaited hair and know they are glad to see me, too. The towels and warm water's ready after Granny sprinkles dried, scented wild geranium in the basin and softly squishes it 'round with her hand. Granny wears her long, worn bib apron, and she carries the precious flowered porcelain pitcher and I carry the bowl into the bedroom. Precious because there is not much lighthearted beauty like this in our hills.

She washes and dries her friend's body without saying a word or shedding a tear. Her touch is sure and swift. She motions for my help with the layers of black clothes sitting on the chair. When almost all is done, she softly calls for the man of the house to pick up his wife and place her in the pine coffin waiting in the parlor, a coffin he most likely made during the night. We follow at a distance to give him a moment alone. After a time, he rests her in the box with a worn quilt for a lining and a small, newly-stitched pillow.

Granny ties the plain black bonnet with the long ribbons securely under the chin and places a penny on each closed eyelid. The family sits stiffly on hard, wooden-backed chairs waiting to say their goodbyes.

We leave without anyone noticing. "Granny, why tie a bonnet on her?" I ask.

"We has to so her mouth stays closed and the pennies keep her eyes shut."

GRANNY'S PRAYER

Lord, take my hand, lead me home,
one more time, before I die.

Back to the green, green grass
on high woody hills in Kentucky
where I was born.

It's been many a year since I
moved away with my family
but the heartache of leavin's
never left my breast.

Roam with me up and down
the rugged slopes and cling to
me along the stone-cropped
ledges where I once played.

Let me run through the flower-
laden meadow and raise me up
over the fence before Rascal,
that old bull, horns me.

Give me a last taste of golden brown
fried chicken, creamy white gravy,
homemade butter on flaky high biscuits
and strong sorghum molasses to start my day.

Walk with me down the hill to my
little worn gray church, hear me sing
ever' verse of *The Old Rugged Cross*
with them saints and sinners.

Come with me Saturday night
when the fiddlers set their fiddles
afire with the fastest playin' you
ever did hear, while we clap hands.

Stand by my side when we come upon
Mt. Hope, where I can sit a spell with
my mama and daddy arestin' in the
ground under the climbin' red roses.

Skip along with me over the rocks in the
creek that winds down to the big river,
its banks thick with scrubby bushes
and cattails tall as me.

Stay with me when we find the ole
homestead buried in a watery grave
a long time ago by those who thought
they could tame the river.

Give me a hoe and let me scratch
that good earth where I'd once again
plant corn, beans, and potatoes so
many's a soul could eat for days.

Lord, I reckon I ask too much,
this body's worn out,
I know your will will be done.

SUNSHINE ANGEL

Elusive as a sunbeam
dancing in the wind.

Evanescent as the foamy
wings of the sea.

She was a bright silver ray
that warmed my path.

White heat with
a promise of heaven.

I tried to catch her song,
hold her still.

But there are spirits
not meant to be silenced.

A fleeting glimpse
of what was meant to be.

She slipped through my fingers
like water through a sieve.

Every time I thought
she was mine she was not.

A SOLDIER'S LETTERS AND SILENT THOUGHTS

Greetings Son of America
There's a far away land calling.
Your brothers are dying, and
your country needs you.

Pack up your house, stow the sticks
of furniture, sign the power
of attorney, say goodbye.

A one-way ticket awaits you.
The gates of Ft. Wayne,
your long journey begins.

Wear stifling woolen blues, hoist your
weapons high, and settle in your web
seat for high-flying hellish hours.

But President Kennedy promised married
men would not be drafted. I didn't burn
my draft card and I didn't run
to another country.

First stop, Chu Lai, South Vietnam,
build a city with the Seabees and
dodge as mortars fly over your head.

Darling Husband
The minutes in a day are like years;
our home is in shutters, and life is lonely
without you.

The flowers you sent
are a beautiful reminder of the way it was
and will be the day you return.

When will this war end? We see the body bags
go by in trucks every day. So many die
and the count goes up and up. I'm afraid
for you and me.

≠

Beloved Wife
Bless the ham radio operators
who share their lines, so I hear your
voice between the *rogers* and *overs.*

The tinkling sound echoes in my ears
long after the last *over,* and my heart
aches with each beat for you.

Will I see you again? The long days
and nights drag on and on.
Rain never stops, and I wade ankle deep
in muddy brown water.

≠

Dear Favorite Uncle
How are you? I miss you. When will
you come home? Today I had ice cream
and cake for my birthday. I'm eight now.

I go to camp next week. My bag's all
packed with candy. I get to sleep in a tent.
          XXOOXX

What I wouldn't give for ice cream!
The beer's always warm, if I get any. It's

over a hundred degrees in the shade every day
and cockroaches play in the bread.

I'm here sleeping under my poncho
in a trench I carve out of dirt
on Colco Island. Dragon Lady's gone.
She was spirited to safety long ago.

Relocation Orders

Next stop Hue, old Imperial Capital
of Vietnam. Build a bridge on the Perfume River
that crawls with fish, snakes, and people.

I hear of a riot at home in the streets of Detroit
while I'm here in a war gone wrong. Who
watches over my wife and family?

Dear Son

Everyone's fine here at home and prays
for your safe return. The National Guard
keeps watch on downtown buildings as we drive by.

Your dad and brother work hard to hold
your business together. I'll send chocolate
chip cookies tomorrow.

Thank God they watch over my beloved
and keep her out of harm's way. Armed
soldiers standing on street corners and
atop bridges at home are hard to believe.

I hope Dad remembers to watch out
for low bids on the tough jobs
and collects the money up front.

I'll be lucky to get a cookie
or two when that package comes.

$\neq$

Orders for Home
Your time here is over. Pack your duffle bag
and hop aboard the silver jumbo jet
parked under cover. You're going home.

I helped build it, but the cost is more
lost lives and a score of wounded
when the Tet Offensive shakes our world
as we escape out of country.

I'm damn lucky. I'm on my way home
and hope that peace awaits me. I leave memories
of war behind, memories of the dead buried deep inside.

HIGHWAY CROSS

Why
lovely Lena
innocent one
the
sunshine lass
with
shining eyes
Who were you and where were you traveling all alone,
your path crossed by those who know, and those who wonder.
why
heaven's highway
found a
loved child
and
made a
sad heart
from a
story sorry
why
we
miss you
winged angel
of the
grassy slope
beneath
grief relief
etched cross
why

HANDS

In infancy
God graced
arms
with a pair
of hands,
so soft
and lithe.
Ten fingers,
five together
in harmony,
all with
shields.
To hold
all
life's beauty
and
push
away fear.
To capture
moments
of repose
and
release snared
dreams.
Gloved,
they
protect
and
do battle
with an
iron fist.
Laced
and
steepled
in prayer,
precious
hands
unite.

FREE FALL

Cell phone? *Check.* Camera? *Check.* Seashell bag? *Check.* Cup of coffee? *Check.*

I'm armed with the trappings of a beachcomber's life and follow the breaking sound of waves lapping at the shore. The sky lights up as the sun peaks through darkness with striking pink and white streaks of soft color traveling across the water. Anticipation mounts because every day brings an unusual seashell, and I've been looking for sand dollars since we arrived several days ago.

My eye's on the sunrise as my hand seeks my camera deep in my pocket. Suddenly there's nothing beneath my foot. My endless step goes on and on and on. A fleeting realization flashes in my mind. Earth has lost its grip on me. I'm floating in an arc like someone doing a graceful ballet. I hear a loud pop as I collapse in a heap on the ground. My shaking hand still holds my coffee cup.

Wow, it feels like when I sailed over my handlebars on the trail bike a long time ago. I landed on my shoulders in soft sand and scrambled to my feet. There were no popping sounds that time.

Embarrassed and stunned, I sit here and think *I want to go home.* Not home to the travel trailer we are in, but home to Michigan, a long way from the Texas shore. Not possible for the moment.

So logic sets in. I'll try walking over to the steps leading to the walkway, and then if it's okay I'll go on to the beach. My foot doesn't feel right, like it's disconnected from my ankle and beginning to ache.

I fish my cell phone out of my pocket and hit 2 for my husband's cell phone. Ever since 9/11, cell phones have become constant companions for us when we're separated.

He drives across the grassy park in his Ford Lariat and skids to a stop in front of me. After scooping me up in his arms, he places me in the truck and tucks a blanket under my foot, which is beginning to look like a football as he carefully removes my shoe and ankle chain.

A handsome young doctor dressed in sweat pants and sandals orders x-rays. His diagnosis is severe ankle sprain and advises it will take four to six weeks of rest, ice, compression and elevation to recover. I'm relieved to know it isn't broken.

My beachcombing days are over for now.

Crutches? *Check.* Air ankle brace? *Check.* Ice pack? *Check.* Vicodin? *Check.*

MAKER OF MEANING

I just want to stare into space
in a special place alone.

Some followers won't let go
mesmerized by my blankness.

Others want to connect the dots,
draw a picture on the canvas.

Believe me, I'm in a serene space
holding on to illusions.

Listen to the quiet of my mind,
seeking always seeking.

My being is not idle; it tosses words
around like the wind tosses leaves.

Thoughts hurtle before me,
collide and come together.

I decipher the moment,
delve into the meaning.

Some of my innermost thoughts
are not meant to be shared.

Give me a pen; I will try
to capture what is born in my struggle.

I'll tell you just enough but
won't defend my thoughts.

I'll give you the basics; you
use your imagination.

Just like in life, you will know
just what you learn, build on what

you understand, experience
what touches you,

but not from what I say
or don't say.

SATIN SHEETS

create a beggar
out of my being,

an endless search for
strokes of passion,

a yearning for
silken skin,

coolness for a
fevered brow,

escape from
fitted layers.

LOOKING BACK

After the longest search, I found you sitting in a junkyard. You were dented, wrinkled in all the wrong places, and your dark navy blue paint was scratched. I circled you slowly, mentally noting the damages: the tattered, red pin-striping, the shattered windows, the hanging tail pipe. When I slid behind your wheel, I felt the coolness of the once-sleek red leather seat and its welcoming contours hug my body.

Inside, I felt like I had come home. I pushed in your lighter, opened the glove compartment and slammed it shut, adjusted your seat to my satisfaction. I could feel the spring air rush past my face through the cracks in your windows, and I longed to be on the road with you once again.

I thought about the long ago happy times and the near misses we shared as we sped through those early years. I learned to drive in you with your four-speed manual transmission. You sailed with me around hairpin curves at high speeds no sane person would try, but I was young. One time, when we came out of a ninety-degree curve at fifty miles an hour and were still hugging the road, I thought to myself, *Ugly.*

I didn't slow down in you, but I had to leave you behind when I moved on with my life. I never forgot the freedom and the song of your purring engine as I shifted through your gears. Nor did I forget the magical feeling of my hair swirling in long tendrils around my head when your top was down.

Now I've come back, and I find you, Sunbeam Alpine roadster, have been waiting for me. I thought life was over when I reached forty, but I've found, with a little bit of paint and hard work knocking the bumps out and polishing the rough edges, we're both good as new.

SOMEONE WATCHES OVER ME

I choose the pink raft, my favorite color. This trip is a sunshine vacation gift for my college graduation. On this magnificent day I'm on Miami Beach. The warm water invites as I dip my toes in first and duck under the waves for a quick submersion before I jump on.

The sun has heated the plastic, and it envelops me in warmth. I close my eyes and feel like I'm floating on a cloud. For the moment I have no fear of the water with so many others around. I remember my mother's story of how I almost drowned when I fell off the dock. I often think my fear of water is brought on by that narrow miss and is now buried somewhere deep inside me, although I can't remember falling in the lake.

I'm three years old, bending over the edge, when I get too close and fall head first off the dock. My daddy pulls me out of the water and hugs me tight. Mother screams at Daddy to watch me closer. As I grow my cousins tease me. If I keep my head above water I won't be scared. I like to stand up with my feet dug into the sand beneath the water. As long as I can do that I feel safe.

We visit my cousins, Kyle and Callie, often at their lakefront home, and if I want to join them I have to go out to the raft moored a short distance from their dock. They never fail to tell me it's okay to stand up as I near it, and I sink below the surface with my hands grabbing for the inner tube they throw me. They think it's very funny, and I try to hide my fears and tears as I dog paddle toward them. I can float, too, but most of the time I just sink.

I open my eyes after a while and—oh, my,—I'm so far away from the beach; it must be a mile between the sandy shore and me. The sun-worshipers look like little ants on the horizon. How did I get so far out? There's hardly a wave. No one else is near. Fear grips me, and in my frenzied attempt to turn the raft around, I topple off.

My first thought: I can't see the bottom. I can't stand up with my head above water. There is no bottom where I am. Panic mounts as I frantically grab for the raft. Water closes over my head, and I don't like it. I hate it. I fear it. A heavy pressure pushes me down and down. My long hair swirls up and around. I can't see. I can't catch my breath, and I feel like a kitty trying to claw its way out of a burlap bag that's been heaved over the side of a boat.

I flail my arms and kick my feet at unseen creatures below. Daddy? My right hand shoots to the surface, and the rest of my body follows as if someone yanks me up and out. There's no one here, not even an inner tube. The raft is only a few feet away from me but seems like a thousand feet away as I dog paddle in that direction.

I feel an eternity pass before I haul myself back on top and feel the warmth kiss my body. I'm too afraid to move and lie spread-eagled on the raft with my fingernails clutching the edge, the endless blue sea spread out before me. *Turn around* whispers echo in my mind. My heart races and exhaustion invades my limbs.

Relax, paddle with your left arm and kick with your left leg is my mantra. Now I head in the right direction—to the beach. With little energy I slowly propel myself onward until my feet feel the scorching sand.

Thanks, Daddy, for not letting go.

CHRYSALIS

Dinah Lee

I know why I was afraid. If I let the words form and tumble onto a page, I believed my stories would be real, and I would have to deal with harsh truths. I didn't know about the healing part of the telling, how it finally feels like the best part of living when you no longer worry about being judged or minimized by the stories.

I kept the stories hidden for a long time, all the while stacking up titles for one day. While the stories were busy taking shape, I was safe. If I didn't complete the tale, I could stay tucked away in the shadows, secretly turning the titles over and over, double-dog daring myself to begin.

It's funny, but telling the stories was somehow telling on myself, outlining some of the choices I'd made, and not being able to take any of it back. But getting the stories out is facing the fears. Choices—good and bad—help us grow. They are each pieces of the whole and don't have to define us. My stories are about hidden choices, defining choices, choices that have moved through me and gotten me here.

There is exhilaration in beginning; as words join hands to weave a story, fears untangle. It's the best part of storytelling, the freefall into the museum of stories, the raw music of souls laid bare. Words come together and lift the page to meet the telling.

To me, everything has a title possibility in it: the amusing things good friends say to hear me laugh, the places I go with sorrow, the discovery of a tasty recipe, the way the wind moves in the pines, and the way my big red dog winks on command. For me, the stories all begin with a title. They find me and tease me forward.

Try this:

If you struggle with the beginning of your story, start with a catchy title, if that's all you've got, and begin to weave your story. Let it be a clever, amusing title, an irresistible pull into what comes next. The words will follow the idea. In my story, "The Queen of Diddley Squat," I wrote about losing a spelling bee, but I carried that title around for weeks before the story came. Feel good about the stories you will tell. Let the title help you begin. Give your life a voice, one title at a time.

IT ALL BEGAN IN THE CLOSET

I would push aside the lime green formal and the boxes of summer sandals, prized but out of style, and open the box at the very bottom that hid the treasure. A flashlight with batteries that, if found by inquisitive brothers, would be stolen to light up the eyes of a plastic dragon. They didn't know I had it. They didn't know I had it in me, either. No one knew. My secret writing shadow was locked up tight, having become such a part of me I was frightened to set her free. Who might I become? Would I be more myself with the freedom, or less, minus the inescapable burden?

I always saved scraps of paper, half-used memo pads, and broken pencils with pieces of lead so small I'd have to write with the lightest touch and take out some words to make it last to the end of the story.

Some pencils had erasers so worn the metal rims they sat inside would gouge holes through my mistakes, reminders of my inability to get it right the first time.

Mom would try to catch me at bedtime, as I waited until the very last second to put the flashlight back in the box, readjust the marks of dust to look untouched, lunge across the room, dive under covers, shove my sister over on her own side, and will my breathing into normalcy. Then I'd hear, "Do I have to come up there? Now, GOOD NIGHT!" The hard click of the hall light was the ultimate signal that Mom was mad as a wet hen and on her way up to see about things.

Years later, after silent light switches were invented, that was the first place my mom installed one, at the bottom of those Godforsaken stairs. The sneak attack the soundless switch allowed gave Alana and me little time to get things back in order before she was upon us. We got very good at anticipation, straining to hear the slightest muffled footsteps signifying *the warden is fast approaching!*

Once I was in such a hurry I forced the flashlight back in the box but left it on in my haste. The next night, when I snuck deep inside my writing cave and prepared to astound myself with memories, my flashlight was dead. It was then I knew I needed to babysit neighborhood kids if I wanted money to buy more batteries.

Shrouded in secrecy, I already knew I'd have to hold some money back and nonchalantly question my brothers about where to buy batteries when the time came. Any appearance of inquisitiveness could bring destruction, so sneakiness was bred in early and vital to survival. I got fifty cents an hour to walk the neighbors' smallest children while the mommies napped, flopping in an exhausted heap, or had a good cry until they saw the returning buggy come back around their corner. I quickly worked seven days a week on our street alone and never came back early. I earned every penny, and the mommies got vicious about protecting the service. We had to account for all money earned in our house, so siphoning off a nickel here and there for batteries was tricky and private.

When things were really bad between my parents, I would try to shrink down very small and hide under the covers. That was not the best plan, as I still left a lumpy ridge beneath the patchwork quilt, a conveniently outlined diversion for their anger. The closet was a better place to hide when my parents were arguing and distracted, and staying hidden at least provided me the company of my characters. Stories would click in my mind, bravely gathering momentum in my safe place, daring me to let them out.

I tried to hide the flashlight under my pillow a few times, balance on my elbow, and write all bent up and crooked in a half-pose under the blanket, but my hair got mashed. When I pulled the covers back, sparks showed in the darkness, messing up my concentration and distracting me with how cool that was. It was a difficult balancing act anyway, and the writing was fragmented and messy. It was always best to avoid trouble by lying low, and the muted light beneath the covers identified the obvious form of a sleepless child and became a target for my parents' moods. If only I could have laid low enough to melt into the sheets, I might have gotten to write more stories, but the harsh positioning would choke off the telling and mirror my own discomfort. There was never a corner small enough to hide in, or a place for me to tell the purest stories in the gentlest way.

My first applause came when I wrote a story about a day in the life of a penny. I can't recall the title, but I'm certain it was catchy. I do recall the story being humorous and, though I struggle now to write funny stories, there wasn't much humor back then, either, so I'm not sure where the laughter comes from or gets stored. Perhaps it's in a shoebox in someone else's closet. The entire class clapped and laughed—even the teacher—and I was hooked. Forget being the class clown; I could pull antics with perfectly chosen words and save myself detention if I could just keep enough batteries.

After that, I participated in every writing class offered, except technical writing. I mean, really, who does that? Once I saw my father spend an entire precious Sunday trying to put together a bicycle by reading the directions. We still call it Bloody Sunday. When Ed Sullivan came on that night, Dad was swearing, shaking his head in amazement over the pile of nuts and bolts he'd skipped over. When the whole pile got flung against the far wall, I knew I never wanted any part of those pamphlets, so frightened I was to miss a step.

In school, Miss Lanew told me that I had a real flair for the dramatic and that every life event could tell a story. That opened up the possibilities even more, as writing my stories had merely meant survival to me. If I could just get the stories out, I'd be okay. I was frequently shocked at how some stories emerged. They were usually fear-based then, with distinct, descriptive sentences. The way one beginning led to a totally different ending in such a wild and circuitous fashion left me breathless and motivated to keep working. Each time I'd earn another handful of coins but come home complaining about wet diapers and snotty noses, Mom would frown and say, "It's never too early to learn that you don't get something for nothing." Upstairs I'd fly to hide another nickel thinking, "That's it? That's the secret of life?"

Over the years, I've had some writing lulls, perhaps because I still felt the need to hide my efforts. There was also a time when I felt unworthy. I could not afford the cost of living my dream. Besides, I had learned that when things came as naturally as breath they could disappear just as easily. Mom still says, "Life is hard, life is a struggle. Look at me with five kids and few of my dreams realized. Know your place, child. Your story is about endurance."

This winter I had a reaction to medication after surgery, suffering several strokes and altering my memories. The fear of thinking I might have lost my storytelling magic forever has brought me out of the closet.

Now I just worry that I might run out of stories. And then I worry that I won't....

ENOUGH!

When my second brother was born, my mother wanted to name him *Enough!* Yes, *Enough!* with an exclamation point. So when I came along, number four of five, the cast was set. No children for me—ever. After all, if number two was *Enough!* what did that say about me? I imagined Mom naming me *Nonetheless.* I had always liked the complexity of a word that was three words in one.

As we grew, we made excuses for our parents' bad behavior, but we knew we didn't want to pass those angry genes along to the next generation. We wanted the pattern to end with us. We used to say that Dad probably wanted us all, he just didn't know what to do with us once he had us. Was that true, or a childish attempt to find our way?

My oldest brother, Allan, was a paranoid schizophrenic personality, and he absorbed the evil genetic structure of the firstborn. Nature and nurture had both had a say in my brother's destructive behavior. Growing up frightened in a house too full of violent outbursts, I declared to my soul that when it was my turn I would never add offspring to the mix. Enough's *Enough!* I took a pass on motherhood and directed my attention to figuring out why things could be so topsy-turvy in a household Mom tried frantically to level out. All of my life I've asked the question, "Why?"

Of course, we each secretly thought we were the bad seed, sharing in turn the reasons why as we hid under our beds or in the closets of our mottled caves. Each time the house imploded, we'd sift through the rubble till hands touched one another, finding safety in numbers. Knowing each other's secret places by heart, we went there with the slightest hint of raised voices downstairs. Like little robots, we would clear all accumulated mementos of life from our dressers and hide them in drawers to keep them safe. Once the raging commenced, the destruction of life overtook all good memories.

Mom didn't name her second son *Enough!* after all. David was a savior to us girls, bigger than we were, and willing to stand up to the monstrous menace once he grew some and gained height and his own version of hostility. David tried to be the protector, even of Allan, and while the house was burning around him, he would try to snuff it all out.

When my older sister grew up, she started early on a family of five, trying to convince Mom that she, indeed, knew the suffering and struggle Mom had gone through to raise the five of us. No longer could Mom tell her oldest daughter that she didn't understand the hardships of raising five children alone. The familial virus was passed on. My sister's life has been one of forlorn dramas and twisted lessons learned. Her beautiful family now shares the legacy, each one mired down, yet ever reaching for the sun.

My turn. When I was fourteen, I was raped by a schoolmate. Grateful that the outcome did not include pregnancy, I dealt with the myriad of feelings with sick gratitude for small blessings. At sixteen, I fell in love with a guy who did everything with me but have sex, but still I thought somehow I had gotten pregnant. I was working at a one-room doctor's office, riding my bike to and from work after school and throughout the summer. She was an obstetrician/gynecologist with cupboards full of free samples of drugs and birth control pills, thousands of them. I began to pilfer my own supply, trying to get up the nerve to take them so I'd be safe enough to humor my boyfriend with sex I wasn't ready for, but sure that was what it took to keep him. Once when my period was late, I spent a crazy afternoon alone in the doctor's office, forcing my pelvic region against every sharp corner in the room—the doctor's desk, the countertops, the equipment sterilizer. Frantic and spent, I thrust myself against one last surface and heard a gushing force of air, a release in my abdomen, and somehow I knew I was safe again.

I can't explain how I knew I didn't want promiscuity to define me, yet even as it became clear to me that it was part of my identity, I fought it. I was all mixed up, thinking that sex was how you caught a man, trapping him in a lariat of sweat and heaving and love, roping him in for all eternity. But eternity's fickle in youth—and fleeting. Sex soon became a dirty prize, misconstrued and darkened by lies.

In one of my college classes, I met a radical guy with a cobra tattoo on his forearm. I was transfixed, fascinated by its poised attack position, so visible and sinister. He was always late, sneaking in the classroom's back door with his shoulder-length, hippie hair and cigarettes rolled up in his T-shirt sleeve. When my friend showed an interest in him, I set out to snare him first. He was a bad boy, but he was funny and attractive, and I had to have him. Plus I fell in love with the image of a struggling couple: he in his stylish "thinking man" glasses and me working late to support his dream. Later, when I married at twenty-three, I thought children would inevitably be in my future. As Mom had taught us girls: when you're married, that's what you do. All she'd ever wanted was to be a stay-at-home mom—a good mom. When her dream never materialized, I compensated by linking myself with a wisp of golden thread directly to her womb. My husband was in medical school, and I was working full-time plus logging in all the overtime hours I could. I clung to an image of being a successful doctor's wife, laying out his handsome husband outfits and lab coats, and starting to live our dreams together. But that never materialized. He began hitting me. He had actually hit me once in the face before our wedding, but that one was clearly all my fault. The hitting continued, but he never left visible marks, so what couldn't be seen didn't count. Then he had a nasty affair under my nose and under my homemade wedding quilt. By then I was pregnant. When we told his mother, she glared at me, saying, "Oh, great! Now you've gone and done it, trapped my baby boy forever. That's the LAST THING you two needed—EVER!" I still didn't get the message, not totally.

I had some semblance of confused remorse when I lost the baby early on and flushed it down the toilet before I thought to scoop it out and show it to someone. I dreamt for months afterward about a baby boy with a snake tattooed on his forearm, swirling round and round in my restless images of toilets and water and drowning, winding up in the sewers near our home, whispering to me and wrestling for a life he wanted me to want for him.

I went to the doctor after my divorce and asked for a hysterectomy. I wanted to end the option of childbirth once and for all. It was the early 80's and women still didn't have rights over their own wombs or life choices. Flabbergasted and appalled, my doctor couldn't fathom my decision and, as was required by law for single women with such a determination, I was told I had to write a letter outlining my intentions. "You're a young, vibrant, single woman. Why, you could meet a man who changes your mind! You've got your whole life ahead of you. Certainly, motherhood is part of your dream …?" It wasn't enough that my reasons were clear to me; I had to substantiate them and have them on file in his little rat-hole office forever. "Who needs to know?" I mewed plaintively. "Isn't it *enough* that I have never been more sure of any one thing in life?" The patterns woven so clearly were unraveling while I lay upon that chilling table, wide open to the opinions of strangers. I wrote the damned letter, a declarative of such finality that it served to remove much of the shame of the act, for the most part anyway.

Whenever people would tell me what a great mom I would've been, I would pause, remembering that letter crammed in a moldy box of history and sigh, sure all over again that I had done the right thing—for me. I would squelch the wonderings of whether or not I would have been the kind of mother my own mother had wanted to be, terrified that I could've ever considered her fate overlapping my own, with children suffering under the debris of violent trappings. I kept alive my secret rationale, the one sure thing that frightened me the most: what if I'd have hit my children? So when people gave me that apologetic sidelong glance of sorrow for my lost children, I would repeat in my mind the words, *no, no, NO!* Then I would wrestle my breathing and my thoughts back to normal, and proceed.

Later, when my younger sister called me, I knew she was pregnant before she told me. In some familial sense, I felt another struggling future unfolding. She eventually married an older man and had another child. She's a good mother, and her girls are light and funny and beautiful.

Perhaps the pattern can be broken, in spite of the generational lessons cast in cement. I'm not sorry about the choices I've made. I still silently believe I might have been impatient and abusive. I carry anger that I succumbed to the requirements of the times and wrote that God-awful letter of justification about my own body, my own womb, my own vision of my future. Now it seems to pepper my discussions with my sisters' girls about the options life holds and the personal choices they must be ready to make with no one else's legacy intertwined. I try not to lecture them, remembering one thing Aunt Kay always said that still rings true, "People rarely learn from other people's mistakes. They learn their own lessons the hard way, which is after all how we really learn."

Through the struggles, the purifying clarity, the promising tomorrows, I step away from the raw music of my words, polish the broken chains of my personal legacy, and say, "Enough's *enough!*"

THE WATCHDOG SLEEPS

Allan was kicked out of school with nothing in his hand but a pink slip and a pair of pointed scissors. He had been chasing girls on the playground with the scissors, nipping at their skirt hems and poking at their clothing. It was becoming a regular activity that increasingly frightened the staff and all the little girls. When Dad was confronted with his eldest son possessing grave behavioral disorders, he decided to ignore the whole situation for one school year and allowed Allan to return to school the following fall as if nothing had changed. But when the school principal *strongly suggested* that Allan be evaluated before returning to school, he meant what he had strongly suggested. My brother was kept home for one, sour year with no one sane enough to teach him the subjects that would help him live some semblance of existence. He was left home with Dad's extreme verbal and physical abuse, our family teacher of evils. Having a bright yet mis-wired spirit, Allan absorbed the evils like an empty well, filling to the brim and over.

That was the end of Allan's lessons, at least in the public school system. By the time he was psychiatrically evaluated, he was off to Hawthorne Center, where he stayed for much of his youth. At the time, it was common practice to include heavy medication for young, active patients exhibiting anxiety, anger, or acting-out behavior. Allan, having learned from the best, sought to rise to the top.

I remember the hushed whispers and urgent, emphatic declaratives filling my parents' bedroom, seeping out under the closed door and into our bedrooms to disturb our nightmares. Half in and half out of sleep, we'd awaken to dress quietly and alone. We knew the drill. We were heading to the institution to say goodbye again to Allan, who had been over-medicated and was near death. It happened frequently, and each time Mom was alerted, our house was turned inside out while the institution's staff tried to justify the medication and Mom tried to stop the insanity. We would be lined up in a quiet, orderly row in the backseat of the family car. We tried to be as small as possible, invisible even, unharmed by association.

He always lived through it.

Each occurrence was met with familial alarm, but the incidents never ceased. One time, during one of the habitual institution runs, I recall looking at my mother's furrowed brow, set jaw, haunted eyes and white-knuckled grip on the steering wheel. Her voice barely a whisper, she said, "I don't know how we'd ever survive the loss if they killed him." That night, we all tapped in and lost some of life's reservoir. Would death be easier than the nightly watch-dogging of the family? Each sibling was chosen in turn to *sleep lightly enough to hear a pin drop*, ever ready to alert the others, jerk awake and lurch to the very ends of our choke-chains just outside the perimeter of safety.

Would death erase the nighttime skirmishes, the ever-present fear that enveloped us? It sounded easy and welcoming. But when danger passed, Mom might smile again. There were times I lived for that and nothing more.

Allan was drop-kicked through life, one institution's metal, clanging doors and endless rings of keys like the next, and the next. With Allan home briefly between behavioral outbursts and then returned, our lives were lived in fits and starts around him. We were ashamed, always trying to rise above it, and always denying that the shame stuck like something icky to be scraped from the bottoms of our shoes. Neighborhood kids weren't allowed to walk to school with us; their parents told us one bad apple spoils the whole bunch. We were tainted and separate.

Allan's pattern was one of behaving just bad enough to go back and then just good enough to come home. Those were not happy family times; the tension overrode the anxiety and anticipation of the inevitable: the decision to send him back.

It never got easier.

But one time after he'd been home for a spell, Allan got placed in a small town halfway house sitting high on a hill covered with lovely maple trees and run by two spinster sisters and their brother. The roster of house members was painful: young men with cerebral palsy, severe mental retardation, missing limbs and numerous limitations—and Allan. It was so far away that we huddled together at home, wondering among ourselves how we'd get there in time if the call came.

One Sunday we were all invited to observe a recital that the house members had prepared. Allan was so excited, hoping that perhaps Dad would show up for something good for a change. He was sitting on the curb, watching us drive up and counting heads at warp speed—counting all of us but one. Dad never came. It was always Mom, only Mom, and all the siblings in tow. Crestfallen, Allan prepared for his part in the play, excited in spite of himself. Suddenly, I recoiled from the event, feigned carsickness, and stayed behind in the parking lot, lying across the back seat and crying, embarrassed for all of us. I could hear parts of the play, the ill-tuned piano accompaniment, the highs and lows of voices, and the scattered, obligatory applause. I hated myself for not being able to join the family and be part of something that was his in a good way. I just couldn't. Somehow later, I think I was spoiling his event as he had tarnished so many of mine. I stayed back, the family watchdog lording over the premises, chained to history.

The next year, when the phone rang and startled us, we again raced time to meet the reaper. Far and away into the night we raced to hear *the message of the exit*. Through the waiting room's thin walls, we strained to snatch any portion of the sordid tale being recited to my mother by the spinsters. Allan, of course, would have to leave. "But where will we take him?" My mother's plea was left dangling. "Anywhere but here," was all they said. "But what could my son have done that could be so bad?"

Allan had been caught on another playground in a group of boys with a rusty nail, gouging their secret password into a boy's buttock. He was already packed and waiting on the curb, looking distraught and pale as he noticed that, whatever his bad behavior had been, it hadn't been enough to make Dad come and see about him. It was Mom, only Mom, there to absorb the tired news.

Thinking back, there are many obvious reasons for my neglect. We were branded, separated and cast out, our life sentence of humiliation. We wore it, and it owned us, defined us. We were forever destined to lunge at the thick, junkyard dog chains wrapped around our necks.

I struggle to define the fierce love between my brother and me, how remote and yet how vivid the feelings are while growing up in a family where someone is *different*. There are many levels of sadness to this story, so many horrific details, but one thing I still regret is my absence during Allan's performance. I waited in our car alone, swallowed up with fear and shame. Well into the night, darkness overtook how I felt about missing out, and filled me with the terror of marauding housemates scratching at the car windows trying to get me for my tardiness.

But it was my turn to be the night sentinel.

... thankful when the darkness fades, the watchdog sleeps with one eye open....

UNFINISHED

To me, the basement was one more way to get in, to get at us, all those windows and that kindergarten door lock—loose, rickety, and so flimsy it almost advertised admittance. Check, recheck, go to bed, get back up, go down and check again.

Anyone within earshot of our house knew the price of admission to our family carnival and the nightmarish trip through a not-so-fun house. They might check in, but getting out and away was another story. In fact, if we'd known the secret to a safe and hasty exit, we would have taken cuts in line and surely gotten ourselves to safety first. We had lived it longer and deserved it first. The order of the suffering.

Where was my place in that order?

To me, the basement was an unfinished attic, all nooks and crannies and creepy spiders. I can close my eyes and see it through a hazy, gauze-effect, ethereal and liquid yet overlaid with clouded afterthoughts and burden. The effort of recollection pulls my breath up short, leans up high on my neck and cuts off all illusion of easement over time.

It is dis-ease, and that's where it all comes from.

To me, the basement was a trap, all the lawn-mowing equipment, the ping-pong table with the car track and train set on it, the bicycles, the old TV with the miniscule screen and the thousands of books and magazines stacked and toppled all around.

The trap was real and breathing. The trap secured the monster's bait and enticed the hapless children. And the monster ran the home.

He would sit at all hours at a card table set up in the middle of the piles of books playing solitaire and having full conversations, out loud and exclamatory, alone, yet accompanied by hidden demons. The cards were worn into an hourglass shape from repetitive shuffling and dealing and held the body oils of a lifetime of secret cheating of the worst order, the kind of cheating that no one knows about but you.

He set traps and checked them regularly, devising games at our expense. He had collected all those books and valued each one. He collected our reactions, once trapped and released, too, comparing our panicked, frozen expressions to his recollections of appropriate terror. Pass—or fail.

To me, the basement was a botched escape, all those stairs to sprint down two at a time. Building up speed and accuracy required hitting the bottom of the stairs in such a way that any breeze from our movement wouldn't be enough to topple any book piles or ... well ... or else.

If we reached the stairwell unscathed, it also meant we could reach through the rickety door lock and out to freedom.

And if we timed it, rehearsed it, and executed it just right, we were off through the field and over the fences that separated us from the library and books of our own. Only those books were books to borrow and return, no piles, no favorites, no collections ... no personal traps.

To me, the basement harbored panic, all endless chores bargained away among each other in order not to be the one sent down to the basement to bend over and reach deep inside the chest freezer, where the frozen loaves of bread were stacked in rows, just like us, awaiting their cold destinies in the family of seven. We would peek around all the hiding places—behind the furnace and air ducts and in the dark, bleeding corners of the trap—sure the freezer lid would bang us unconscious while we teetered precariously on its edge, scratching for the first clutch of chill our fingertips could claw away from the others to clamor backwards and out, breathing less harshly, but not yet restored once our toes felt the concrete floor signaling safety. "I'll wash your dinner dishes for a week if you'll go down and get the loaf of bread Mom wants," we would earnestly beg one another. Each alert to the ripple of panic, we negotiated the stakes and one-upped considerably. And it was well worth it. Even one less trip to the basement and the freezer meant victory, tragedy averted, gobbling panic staved off for another day.

To me, the basement was a glance into a festering wound, all oozing and needy and confused, getting past the monster and the piles of books and the chest freezer's frozen rows of bread and the spiders and the unfinished business and the breathlessness. It meant not looking over at the piles of sorted laundry next to the freezer, more crumpled traps set out and around at the bottom of the laundry chute with its downward spiral of soiled outerwear, the blues and whites and assorted colors stacked and heaped and stained and neatly piled up like so many loaves of bread, one flowing into the next, all toppling over on us and cutting off our breath, waiting to capture us and suck us down....

NOT-SO-HOT PANTS

I remember thinking afterward how odd it was that I'd never gotten to take off my coat, as if my mind needed to turn the experience into a social event of some sort in order to deal with it on any level.

I was fourteen, pristine and intact. Like all the other kids, my sex education to date had consisted of little pencil drawings in the margins of *The Human Anatomy* book at John F. Kennedy, Jr., Library. Giggling, I hushed away with my girlfriends to the farthest corner, surrounded by shelves of dusty books and gaped at pictures of a boy and a girl dissected for all to see. So, of course, we thought we'd seen it all. This was the real deal, and it was fascinating. We'd discuss sex with exaggerated knowledge one moment, then collapse into convulsive snorting about it right after. As much as our mothers had prepped us for *the devil* to pay his monthly visits, we knew the subject of sex was truly off limits with them. Asking for information meant we wanted to do it, or wanted to be sure to do it correctly, or knew someone who had done it, or we had already done it and now *the devil's visit* was late. Regardless of the level of so-called expertise, asking any questions *whatsoever* meant there would be one fewer kid sporting hot pants at Friday night's talent show.

Mom was such a good seamstress. She would pick lovely material for the outfits, even though they were to-the-knees versions of maternal compromise. I could attend the Talent Show in them all right, and I could even enter the Hot Pants Contest, but you could bet the winner would have mile-high legs and a hint of cheek showing, not a hint of knee.

There I was, entering the decorated gymnasium with the *Back to the 50's* theme, wearing a Catholic school version of the latest fashion statement and surrounded by my friends. Each girl sported the same straight, long hair parted down the middle with bangs, each had dancing eyes and a head bobbing to the beat, and each was coated early with a fine sheen of perspiration as a hint of things to come. We were out, we were together, and we even had permission. We looked cute and young and hip and happy. We busied ourselves adjusting things and settling in, looking around for the boys.

Later, as the fun wound down, we synchronized our watches and headed toward our curfew. We piled into the car of the only friend who had a license, squeezed in like circus clowns, all of us sweaty and full of happy, tired sighs, and prepared to start dropping each kid off at home. Cindy and I settled into the backseat cushion, knowing we lived furthest away from school and would be dropped off last. A boy sat between us that we knew from school. He had placed second at the talent show with a band that played Jimi Hendrix music. The guys were all calling him *Little Jimi* after the way he'd jammed on the lead guitar with an air of future rock star that made me notice him.

I had to go to the bathroom long before we reached his house, so when he offered me the use of his, I gladly accepted. I raced down a long hall straight to the bathroom with him shouting *last door on the left* at me. I vaguely noticed the closed wooden door leading to his bedroom on the right, first door inside the house. Coming back down the hall toward him, I was ready to thank him, congratulate him again for his second place trophy, and leave with a *see you Monday!* when he grabbed the sleeve of my coat and pulled me inside.

I can recall the escape mantra I clung to, repeating over and over in my mind, *If you live to tell about it, you'll be okay. If you live to tell about it, you'll be okay ... please oh please don't mutilate me anywhere that shows....*

It happened fast—or slow—I'm not sure which. It was bloody, painful stabbing, hitting the bulls-eye, missing the target, a pierce, a poke, a thrust. His breath smelled of stale cigarettes and Doublemint gum, a harsh assault of groaning, forceful air directly in my face. Yet each time I tried to turn away, my lips scraped across his shoulder and I could taste his day-old, salty sweat mixed with the taste of panic. The whole time I willed myself to focus on my mantra, drowned out everything else, smothered everything lifeless, even the honking horn in the driveway, the car full of school friends waiting to go home.

"There, I'm done with you," he said with a totally self-absorbed grunt. I knew I was still whole then and prayed to God that it was over. I had chosen complacency, hoping that later, at home, I would show no visible signs of struggle. *Wait, why hadn't I struggled again? Right, right, the mantra, the release, get through it, just get through it.*

I felt then that he'd done this before. It was the way he'd claimed his right, declared his possession, branded my flagging spirit. Everything that had ever made sense to me was traded in that night for Little Jimi's second place trophy.

I mumbled something guttural and incoherent, swiped away tears, and tripped toward the car outside. I was ashen and discarded and changed forever. Cindy thought I was disheveled because I'd waited too long to use the restroom. She scolded me for taking so long, and we squealed back out of the driveway to make up time. When I got home, Mom, who agreed because I'd met my curfew, let me spend the night at Cindy's.

Later, when I showed Cindy my torn and soiled panties and tried through gulping sobs to explain my behavior, she got angry because now I'd had sex first.

I knew then that I knew nothing about anything.

That night, I traded my wonderful hot pants outfit to Cindy for her Beatles notebook. It was a fair trade, too, since she didn't understand the urgency of the trade. She wore my tarnished hot pants that weekend to her cousin's birthday party. I don't recall my Mother ever asking why I'd worn the new outfit only once.

"Well, what were you wearing, dear?" was the question I was afraid someone might ask. I thought I was braced to discuss it, I really did, as if the garment choice of the victim determines her fate. Beforehand, I had thought myself brave and spirited. My best friend's response willed me to keep it all to myself. I caught myself rehearsing my response, ready to defend not my honor but my outfit.

If asked, I could say, "I was wearing my pretty, new, hot pants outfit, the one with the lush, colorful flower print and the *handsewn by Mother* tag at the nape of the neck" or "I was still in my new, royal blue, faux fur winter coat. I never got to take it off. Please quit looking at me that way. Believe me, life can be altered in an instant with your knees nearly covered and your coat still on...."

Even though my answers were now laced with illusive innocence, I never let them out. I kept still. Through the racing heartbeats and the ill-chosen friends, I kept still. Through the future of poor choices and botched decisions, I kept still. I looked at life through the gauzy sleeves of my homemade dresses and kept still.

In my first hour class on Monday morning, I saw him loping across the front lawn of the junior high school. He was with a buddy, tardy and carefree and laughing easily. My ears began to ring. I felt myself swaying in my seat. Someone was holding my head underwater, and my vision got blotchy.

"Well, what were you wearing, dear?" Funny how later I still anticipated that question. As if wardrobe choice could ever justify the chronic shivering, the bent and lowered head, the isolated distortion of even the simplest decisions. *I remember what I was wearing when I got my first bicycle at eight years old. Let me tell you about that outfit. I remember the new hip-hugger jeans I wore two years ago to a party after school. But you probably just want the details of that outfit. Why did we ever call them hot pants, for crying out loud?*

I didn't know that to talk about the experience was to heal, that the judgment of others encompassed far more than their opinions of that one act. I blamed myself and swallowed my future in chunks of shame. If only I'd struggled, if only I'd been marked up as testament to my fight, if only I'd felt I could tell someone, I might've changed the course of fate. But after that happened to me, I could never figure out how to start the conversation. Not with anyone.

ONLY FOUR

Before a psychopath becomes a serial killer, there is that first victim, the beginning of the series, the one that's just going along tracing dreams and living life, the less cautious one, the first.

And people living around that fear, hugging their children and their own knees tighter than yesterday, don't even realize who's lurking among them. Not yet. That first one doesn't get noticed right away, and not by everyone, either. It's still a fluke, lunchroom chitchat, idle grist.

Then the second one happens, within spitting distance of the first, and it is now just plain unfortunate. How unlucky. She must not have been paying attention. Where were her parents, for heaven's sake? Her family must not live right, must not watch closely enough, like we do. Did it happen while the kids were swinging in the yard and their mother couldn't resist running in to silence that ringing phone? Was it really less than five minutes overall, before she understood the life-altering insanity of distraction?

Details begin to come out, circumstances of the events define each child. The children take on names, we see their pictures, we prickle with the early stages of being more aware, more frightened. We walk our children to the bus stop and ask them three times if they've got their cell phones. We take them to the local fire department on fingerprinting day and, to help hold back the swelling tides of fright, we fib about the reason for such a thing. We cling to the belief that it doesn't happen in little, sleepy hometowns. Monsters like the bigger cities, where kids don't play flashlight tag in dark fields for fun.

Without realizing it, we begin to wait for Number Three. Every mother at every venue looks at every other mother, feels the creepy, crawling spinal fingers that trigger that sidelong glance, the over-stare that searches each face in the crowd for clues, afraid for ourselves, our families and neighbors, and the mothers who've come before us in loss. We wonder what we would do if it were us, and each mother is sure she could not endure it. This is shared family penetration, the upsetting of the nests, the stirring of behavioral adaptations that mark the pattern as it pants and heaves and silently pads into each house in its stalking feet.

We become obsessed as a community, watch the drama unfold, no heinous scar left covered. Over and over we watch, puddling up and spilling over into what the kids are allowed to do. Lock down. Neighborhoods hum until the streetlights come on, everyone's mom is everyone's mom, and all the kids feel punished. Fear doesn't register the same in youth. The concept of prey is nebulous and faint.

We know by the maps we've seen on the news where each body was dumped, each colored pin represents a ravaged soul. Bushy shadows by the garage are monsters to us now, and the book-bags the kids carry are getting lighter. Mothers with vans converge on the milling children waiting for the bus, insist they all tumble in together, and as the sun rises they pray for any normalcy that school might provide. Kids tell each other they're afraid of being snatched up, but they're unsure of what that means, really. They steal down the stairs at night and snatch up pieces of adult conversation from the kitchen, rendering them unable to go up to bed in their own rooms. They'd prefer curling up with a sibling. It might not be just for tonight. This is now a series.

There are four.

The questions come like flood waters, the *why? why? why?* Every person within sight of the headlines tries to grasp the meaning of random terror. We search for visible patterns to shield us in our unsettling scenery. If we can decipher the aberrant behavior, we can assure the masses and settle back into our own hurry and our private, tiny spaces. Evil saturates our sanctuaries; we recheck our doors at night and get spooked easily if we take a shower while home alone. We are accustomed to our vulnerability during sleep and nakedness, but now we wonder who might be watching, how he might see in, and what he might see. We fear for our secrets and their disclosure. We keep our big dog close.

With this last one, lives unravel. I know her. The details are my story, the photos on the newsstand come from our family album. I was there for her birth. She got straight A's in school, had big college dreams, and a part-time job for pocket change. She played the flute. Her baby-doll face was carved from sweet beauty, and her heart was kind and dear. She loved her family and was very funny. She used to play dress-up with old jewelry, big hats and fur stoles to play the homespun game, *Ask Me Where I'm Going?* with its elaborate storyline of make-believe. Her imagination was charmingly dramatic and full of flair. I spoke her eulogy where no words could shake the lifeless mass.

The life sentence has begun.

The next phase seems obvious; we must gather all the other families together and create an opening in our extended fold. They are you and you and you, no longer unrelated. It is untrue, safety in numbers, for we find we're all holding our collective breath for either the end or the next one. It is too late for us either way, as the shattering has already engulfed and swallowed each ancestral morsel. Every one of our bodies is now punctured with colored pins, and our life leaks from each hole. The telltale signs of sleeplessness gaze out at a world that shivers in the gray and murky chill. All is cement and heavy. The ache of sameness marks each day like the last. No fine lines identify the puzzle, the blur is a bottomless earth.

The merging of each family's separate pain becomes too great, so the members retreat back within their own despair. We see it in the departing faces, the breaking points just ahead for their private sorrow. We know tomorrow will come and wonder how we'll ever see it as anything more than a tainted, blurry smear.

Even after the series ends and the monster occupies a proper dungeon, life returns so slowly it is unrecognizable. What remains are minds boggled by the broken questions and seeping hearts. Every scrap of bloody denim, every photo's fractured lightness, every clue buttoned up and sealed in the archived evidence box parades through our nightmarish hauntings.

During nights of fitful sleep, I kick my husband out of bed with the strength of armies, screaming if he touches me, so certain I am that no prison walls are strong enough to hold back demons. I have become part of the pattern, once removed, for I freeze with fear if I hear hurried footsteps behind me on the sidewalk. I lock up, paralyzed, unable to look back, yet the irresistible urge forces a last minute, reckless glance, just in case danger is nipping at my heels, his raspy breath close in my ear.

"How many did he get?" people ask. "Which girl did you know? You know, I think I remember that one. She was such a lovely young girl. How many were there again? Oh, right, only four … well, thank God it wasn't double digits. You know, these sickos can really go on a murderous spree. But four, hey, that's not too bad.…"

And there it is. What is meant as consoling is dismissive. Only four. After awhile you can no longer dredge up detailed explanations to share with strangers. No amount of detail will serve to keep them truly safe. You keep your burden to yourself and brace for the next one.

THE QUEEN OF DIDDLEY SQUAT

I never dreamed that the smoldering tip of a bad cigar and a boy I didn't know I liked would make me misspell a word. We were going through the final stages of spelling bee trials in school. My best friend, Cindy, had studied with me night after Godforsaken night, coaching, calling out each word, using it in a sentence, sharing its language of origin—anything to help me find the word in my mind and reel it off without a hitch. In fact, she was so anxious for me to win the next round in school that, when morning came and it was her turn to get up on that stage and spell, she purposely misspelled *buffalo*. She knew that word front and back, and I knew she knew, and she knew that I knew she knew. Huh? She bravely and without malice left out one of the *f*s and then turned a light shade of pink and walked off the stage. True friendship was never sweeter.

I was considered a spelling geek, being dyslexic and therefore seeing all words forward and backward. Some letters were upside down and some flipped within the word, yet I was able to spell any word during competition. When I reigned victorious, the feeling was one I was unfamiliar with—*popularity*—and it felt fantastic. Gone were the feelings of inadequacy, the household shouting matches, the dread of always being frightened, and the heavy fear of failing. I could spell and I could be Queen. The Spelling Bee Queen. I was going for the crown!

Round after round sent each of my classmates to the section of the room for misspellers. I was determined not to be one of them, with their little heads down and their hands too fidgety in their rumpled laps. Not me, my girlfriend had taken a dive for me. I owed her. That felt safer than saying I wanted it badly for myself. When it came down to me and Wesley Jones, I noticed that he was surrounded by the cutest girls in school, oohing and aahing over him and making quite a fuss—and not for his spelling abilities. I hadn't noticed that he was that cute before, but all the attention he was sucking from the room was going to leave little for my victory. Frantic and nerdy, I hesitated, no longer certain of my own abilities. I looked for signs from Cindy, a thumbs-up or a half-smile, but she was busy talking. Suddenly I got all confused and felt something come over me that totally threw me. Not knowing what to do with the whole impossible situation, I decided that maybe I had a crush on Wesley. I knew it was nuts to feel that way so suddenly and completely, yet the teenage weirdness genes were spinning around and landing on all my tender places.

Yes, I got up there when it was my turn, stole one quick glance at Wesley and his groupies, and misspelled. His cheering section went into overdrive as I slunk to my seat alone. The foolish grin plastered on his now adorable face clinched the whole thing for me. I convinced myself it was all worth it. Surely he would realize the sacrifice I'd made for love, cut through the crowd straight to me, swoop me up in his arms, twirling me just so, laugh and sparkle and dance in his victory, and make me his forever.

Nothing even close to that happened. He absorbed his adoration and glory for eons, while I slumped in my seat with my little head down and my hands too fidgety in my rumpled lap. I looked around for Cindy to walk out with me, but she was gone and probably good and mad. She had never thought Wesley was cute at all and certainly wasn't going to understand my momentary lapse for love. I had caved—and Wesley was wearing my tiara.

Not to be undone with the intense crush I couldn't shake, I began to follow Wesley around the school. I would hide behind pillars in the hall outside his classes and wait for him to show up before class. Somehow, I would be there when he left class, still hidden, still staring at him and studying his features like the written word. His popularity had soared several notches with his buddies while mine had taken quite an ugly turn. I was determined to regain my self-respect and focus on the next spelling bee, but I couldn't stop thinking about Wesley.

It was a mystery to me that I could isolate my feelings *BW*, or *Before Wesley*, and realize that I'd traded notoriety for stalking. I was everywhere, too, watching him head toward the bathroom between classes, watching him go to and from football practice, and watching him walk home. I was so distracted I was sure I'd never spell again. Cindy, so truly disgusted with my behavior, had deserted my spelling practice sessions altogether. I was crazy in love and all alone.

Somehow I pulled myself together, resting on past memorizations, and entered another school spelling bee. This time I wore invisible blinders and willed myself to look straight ahead and concentrate only on the word. It worked and I won. Of course, Wesley had entered, too, foolishly thinking he now had spelling talent because he'd never realized that I'd taken the fall for him. He was out of the running early, and I must admit I really enjoyed it. It broke the insane crush with a flash of a word and his pissed off glance in my direction, as if his spelling mishap was somehow my fault. As quickly as it had taken me over, it was gone, and Wesley was back to looking average.

I got my crown back and moved up to the State Championships, representing my school as Queen. I could hear Mom begging Dad to take the morning off and support me in my glory. Dad never came to anything, so I wasn't expecting him to agree. "If I'm taking time off work, it'll be for something I like, like baseball or wrestling, and you haven't seen me doing that lately, have you?" he asked repeatedly as he stormed around the house slamming closet doors and getting madder and madder because he couldn't find his decent shoes. I struggled, wanting his support yet figuring he'd somehow embarrass me and take away any hint of happiness I might wring from the day. Mom was enough support; Mom was safe, and she would be happy if I just tried my best.

But along came Dad, muttering all the way to the car, smoking that big, nasty stogie of his. Ernie Harwell was on the radio announcing the baseball game, and the windows were up. We almost got to the end of our street before I threw up in the back seat. The nervous anticipation was too much, and Mom's special Queen for a Day breakfast was history. That ended Dad's support for my day with a flourish. He pumped that cigar to a pulpy mass between clenched teeth, pulled over for Mom to help me in the back seat, and we continued on with the windows cracked some. By the time we got to the school auditorium, I had anxiety, nausea, and a rumpled dress. We were in a different school in our district, and it had an enormous auditorium. I prayed Dad would disappear somehow, as he plopped himself in the middle seat right in front of the stage and directly in my line of vision. No blinders and strength of will would keep me from staring straight at him, the disbeliever, the miserable mutterer, the man who would dare me to fail with his glare.

Round after round disqualified each stranger, each of them dressed nicely with hair slicked back with pomade and parted on the side. The boys wore striped cardigans, and the girls wore patent leather shoes and anklets, dresses with full, swishy slips, and barrettes. The only way I knew Dad was even listening was I could see that bright orange glow of his cigar tip light up whenever I started across the stage toward the microphone. I wished he wouldn't inhale at all, but he was still breathing. I, on the other hand, was panting. I wanted that championship more than anything. Maybe then Dad wouldn't remind me on the way home that I would never amount to anything. He could hardly say that with my crown taking up the entire back seat of our old Ford.

But I'm getting ahead of myself. Students spelled word after word incorrectly, and the chairs on stage emptied. My head was still up, but my hands were too fidgety in my rumpled lap. And each time it was my turn, there would be that glowing cigar tip directly in my line of vision. I was increasingly distracted, and as the morning progressed and there were fewer spellers around me, I had to fight within myself to stay focused on the far wall of the auditorium, high up and over the *head of Dad with smoldering cigar.* I would tell myself before I spelled, *Just look down at him once, just a quick glance and get it over with. Then go on and spell the word.* But he got me, as he always got me in the end.

The word was *CHRYSALIS,* a butterfly as it passes through its pupa stage in a quiescent condition, enclosed in a firm case. That was me, all right, quiescent meaning making no trouble about your condition. I was as quiet as a mouse. The one and only time Dad ever came to anything and I had lost the crown. The whole ride home was silent. I could see Mom in the front seat next to Dad, her peripheral glances and furrowed brow daring him to keep still. But whether he berated me or kept quiet didn't matter. All I could see was that smoldering cigar, glowing brightly in the front row of the auditorium and now in the front seat of the car, as he churned on that soggy stick to keep his peace. If it were possible, I would have thrown up again and gotten rid of the despair once and for all. Bloody rotten *chrysalis*. I knew it was a quiet butterfly enclosed in a case. And I felt six feet under—my wings clipped, my crown stripped of jewels—wishing I could fly away.

BLESS YOUR HEART

Bless your heart. Grandma said it to start every conversation. She'd say *bless your heart* and then ask about the children. She'd say *bless your heart* if you finished cleaning your plate. She'd laugh that glittery, twinkling sparkle of a laugh that joins families to time, the kind of earthy laugh that sinks you back into the tucks and gatherings of the best old memories. She would furrow her brow, shake her head, center her hands on her hips or rest them under her chin, and add a *bless her heart* or a *poor, poor heart* throughout the telling of family stories. It is an enchanting memory still, and every time I hear myself say it, I know I'm saying it for her.

She was a grandma in a grandma's house. Her home was nestled among regal maple trees—on Oak Street—in a neighborhood where every street was named for trees. There were soft places on Grandma's wooden porch where we couldn't stand, spongy areas to walk around or we'd fall through the rotting slats and straight through to China. The house looked more crooked each time we drove up to the curb. But once inside, the smell of hot blueberry muffins in paper cups would stand us up straight, heading for the glass candy dish that was full of round, pink peppermints. We'd carefully work to get the lid off quietly, no last second clang of the glass lid against the dish, or Mom would hear us from the kitchen (how did she do it?) and yell, "You kids get out of that candy dish right now! You'll spoil your dinner, and grandma made you muffins!"

Every picture of Grandma in my parents' wedding album terrified me; she was so enormous. She was made up of layers of flesh and jiggling arm skin that waved when she waved, skin flaps she told us were her wings, and an endless bosom she'd squish us in, gather us close to her heart, and hold us in the protective scent of Evening in Paris cologne and her favorite body powder, Cashmere Bouquet. She wore splashy flowered prints that went on forever and that fine, pure, white, curly hair hidden under a hairnet even then. She had those old lady ankles that swell and flow over the tops of laced, sensible shoes. We used to go to Ben Franklin's, the local five and dime, and pool our nickel allowance money to buy her the most luxurious, dazzling, broaches any grandma ever received. She wore one on every dress, smack dab in the middle of her ample bosom, holding back the lace hanky she always found a nose for, welcoming us into the most joyous place to rest our head there ever was for children needing a soft place to land.

I remember chenille bedspreads on Grandma's beds and my older sister and me wearing our homemade, matching dresses to show off to Grandma. Mom would lift them gently over our heads and hang them on glass doorknobs while we napped in our slips, a special treat reserved only for afternoon naps at Grandma's house.

The antique rocker in the corner of her dining room next to the small, framed window overlooking Grandma's garden was the perfect place to sit. We would nestle in tight with a good book, the light from the reading lamp silhouetting the muted flowers on the wallpaper, rich textures of colored peonies and snapdragons, the accent as warming as her smothering hugs, the rocker creaking like athletic knees. It was a special place to dream, listen to the canaries singing in their brass cages, and breathe in the scent of whatever sumptuous treat was rising in the warm kitchen.

Grandma's house had a wooden stoop from the dining room into her checkered linoleum kitchen, a soft, soothing tapping for our Sunday patent leather dress shoes. Tap, step, tap, step, up, down, over and over, we were fascinated by the muted comfort of the passageway from the front of the house into the beloved kitchen. There was Grandma Almighty, potholders in hand to check the baking, wearing her floral apron with the tie at the neck, enormous pockets with bric-a-brac trim, and wrinkled handprints from wiping flour after lightly dusting muffin pans for church luncheon favorites and anxious grandkids being well-behaved so that we could lick the spoons.

Her Christmas poinsettias were still blooming bright holiday red in springtime and the rickety, leaning wooden fence surrounding her backyard encouraged her breathtaking hydrangeas to re-bloom beyond anything we'd ever seen. Each year my parents would bring her the same lilies at the holiday, and Grandma was as excited as if it were a new car she'd never learned to drive. Her friends all belonged to the Golden Age Club, a name that didn't sound like a bunch of old biddies to us at all, but a clandestine gathering of grandmas in glitter and hairnets and sequins. She spent her entire seventy-fifth birthday pacing from dining room to kitchen and back, fretting and mumbling over and over, "I'm three quarters of a century old, who'd believe it, I'm three quarters of a century old...."

Uncle Jim was Grandma's eldest son, married to Aunt Gladys and living close by in an old farmhouse full of antiques. They had a claw-foot tub at the top of a thousand stairs we raced up and down till parents made us stop, pulling the chain for the light bulb off and on, off and on with a click. We would carry the guinea pigs they raised all around the upstairs rooms, each lit from intimate lampshades that outlined the carved walnut headboards and handmade comforters, side tables that didn't match but somehow fit, and the tiny vases of fresh flowers for guests to appreciate. Uncle Jim had a full-bellied, Santa Claus laugh, and Aunt Gladys' decorating style encouraged my own love of antique furnishings and the stories behind each piece.

Aunt Geraldine, Aunt Geri to us, got struck down with polio early in life but never let it stop her. She would wheel that chair around the house with ease, her cupboards all lowered within reach and an elevator that Uncle Bill put in, going to the basement, so that she could teach ceramics while he poured the molds for classes. She was big and joyous and so rich with love and gentle touches that we would beg to visit her and hear her sing us soft little songs of made-up endearments. *I like you like you are. I wouldn't want to change you, or even rearrange you, not by far ... 'cause I L-I-K-E like you like you are!* When she died, I bent close to her cool ear, held her clasped hands, and sang to her the song that meant so much to me, a verse to carry her up to heaven, to collect her wings and hear my voice echoing in her mind forever.

I always wondered what made Grandma name my dad *George Casper.* For us, Casper was a friendly ghost and cause for a chuckle every time we said his name. I remember Aunt Geri telling us childhood stories about our dad and questioning his erratic behavior and the distance he maintained throughout his early years. Later, when he beat my brothers with a broomstick handle, we asked Aunt Geri why he was so angry and why he would choose such a punishment. She shook her head sadly and replied, "Why, that's what Grandma used to use on him, bless his heart." That was such an incongruous act to us, an internal conflict of behaviors—our beloved, idealized grandma grabbing a broom from the kitchen we cherished and beating her child while remnants of a blueberry muffin were still on his lips.

Dad's sister, Aunt Jean, studied to be a nun but one day snuck out with a boy and, while riding on the back of his motorcycle, raced across the train tracks to beat the train and never made it back to Grandma's. She went to be with the Lord she thought she wanted to marry. We had one picture of her smiling out at us, wearing her matching turquoise necklace and earrings and looking like my sister, Alana. I thought she was so beautiful, someone I wished I could have met. I have drawers of similar jewelry, each bought with Aunt Jean in mind, the matching sets the nieces wear when they play dress-up at my house.

Grandma had a huge belly we thought all grandmas had if they are really grandmas. But Mom said it was from something they called *dropsies,* an ailment she regularly visited her doctor for, a doctor whose name was Charlie Brown, which brought on laughter and disbelief. *No wonder she never got better,* we thought, *with a doctor named from the Sunday funnies.* When she died, Dad came to the funeral. We hadn't seen him in years since the divorce, so it was an impossible day of loss and emotional confusion. The family and all the neighbors brought covered casserole dishes and lovely desserts but, bless their hearts, they were not like Grandma's blueberry muffins.

IN THE GLOAMING

Maryhelen Hagood

In winter, just after dusk, before dark,
the blackened trunk and gnarled branches
of our old oak tree contrast against
royal blue sky and snow. This intense blue
permeates my soul. I see indigo air
in the gloaming.

The natural beauty of my surroundings influences my writing. I continue to live on the lake where my husband drowned eight years ago. Writing has helped me heal from the sudden shock of losing him. Daily, animals and birds, the changing beauty of sky and lake provide me with solace. On some winter days, if proper climatic conditions are present, I see a blue glow reflect off the sky, lake, and snowy ground outside my window. This blue is palpable. When I first noticed it, I remembered a word from an Irish song my mother used to sing, *In the Gloaming.*

I am part of a grand design, connected to my ancestors, descendants, friends and pets, the abundance of plant life surrounding me, the lake in front of my home, a duck who returns each summer to nest in my hollyhocks. This sense of connection sustains me.

I am in the gloaming of my life.

Try this:

Try a metaphor exercise. As you move through life, look for an object, scene, sound or motion that is so beautiful and unusual it suspends time, takes you outside yourself. Compare it to something else, something unexpected, the way I've described *winter air* as *indigo air* or the way I've compared a pear tree to a pregnant woman in the poem, *Ripe Russets.*

ANNIVERSARY PICTURES

I walk into the house smiling,
eager to show the anniversary
pictures to my husband.

My son comes toward me, anguish
on his face, tears in his eyes. He says,
"Something terrible has happened."
"Has your father been in an accident?"
He nods.
"How badly is he hurt?"
"He's dead."

On the way to the hospital, I think,
Nurse anesthetist daughter is with him.
She's brought others back.
He'll be alive when I get there.

But she says, "He's gone."
He looks alive to me.
"If he's dead why
is the cut on his ear still bleeding?"
She answers, "He's losing
his clotting factors."

After awhile my husband tells me,
Quit making crosses on my forehead.
The lake baptized me.
Quit twisting your fingers in my chest hair.
Stop kissing my cheek.
Can't you see my face
is turning purple?
It's time for you to go.

My life is changed forever.

COME BACK

for just a few hours
dance with me
come to my bed.

Once I said, "I married you
because I knew you would
never let me down."

You answered, "I married you
because I didn't think I could
live without you."

Now *I* have to find a way
to live without *you.*

HERE I AM

Here I am, nine months pregnant, stuck in a hospital elevator. My husband frantically pushes the control buttons. I grab hold of the wall railing. My groan turns into a grunt. My husband looks alarmed. "Stop that. You can't have this baby here. I won't know what to do." Speaking through clenched teeth, I say, "You won't have to do much. You've already done your part." With super human strength, he grabs the elevator door and, even though we are stuck between two floors, manages to wrench it open. A loud alarm begins to sound.

He sits on the floor of the elevator and slides down to the floor below, holds out his arms to me, "Jump, I'll catch you." "No." "Come on, Maryhelen, jump." Just then a strong contraction knocks me to the floor. I fall out of the elevator into his arms. "That's my girl! I knew you could do it!" My lips curl into a snarl. I am about to bite him; the contraction eases and I become sane again.

A nurse with a wheelchair comes toward us. "Where have you two been? ADMITTING called fifteen minutes ago and said you were on the way." My husband tells her, "I don't think we should stand around talking. The contractions are coming very rapidly." She wheels me off to the delivery room, muttering, "I'd like to get the person who set the alarm off. It's waking my patients."

Within a half hour I give birth to a beautiful eight-pound boy. The doctor looks for my husband, finds him asleep on the waiting room couch. The alarm still blares.

DINING OUT

It's a beautiful summer afternoon. Norm and I drive north on Woodward Avenue after touring the Detroit Zoo with our five children. We stop at a Howard Johnson's restaurant for dinner. The children are well-behaved during the meal. As we finish up, four-year-old Ricky gets Norm to take him to the restroom. Everything is going so well, I contemplate ordering dessert.

As I try to get the attention of a passing waitress, two-year-old David decides he is through eating and starts to rock his highchair back and forth. At home this behavior gets my attention, and I quickly free him from his imprisonment. On this occasion I'm not quick enough; the highchair goes crashing to the floor. David screams his hurt and outrage.

As I bend down to pick him up, ten-year-old Ginny, always eager to please, jumps up to help—thereby upsetting the table and all its contents. Six-year-old Martha, a slow eater, looks down at her unfinished spaghetti dinner splattered all over the floor and starts to cry. Eight-year-old Katy grabs my skirt and starts sucking her thumb, a behavior she gave up two years ago. Ginny wishes the floor would open up and swallow her. I hold the still-screaming David.

Norm, returns from the restroom with Ricky, calmly assesses the situation and starts to clean up the mess. The waitress comes over and tells him, "No. I'll do it. Please *just leave!*" My entourage and I head for the car. Norm goes to the cash register to pay our bill. He leaves a hefty tip.

DEAR BEVERLY,

Remember how your yard backed into mine?
A fence marked our property line,
kept dogs at home.
You said, "Let's have a gate so our children
can go back and forth to play."

We had swimming pools. You planted flowers
around yours. Sounds floated through the tall
evergreens around mine: music, children's
playful shouts, the baseball game on the radio.
One April I heard you say, "It's not spring
until I hear Maryhelen laugh."

In September I said, "Summer was too short!"
You said, "I'll bet winter will be long."
We moved away, lost touch after a few years
of Christmas cards. When her dad died
my daughter called your home.
Your daughter said, "Mom died two years ago."

Beverly, winters are getting longer and colder.

Love,
Maryhelen

BELOW THE SURFACE

I submerge into a different world.
There is no sound.
The sun's rays refract as they
reach the water's surface
creating geodesic-like designs
on the bottom of the pool; these shimmer
as I move slowly through the water.
Back and forth I swim,
mesmerized by this world.

I have tried these fins, this mask
and snorkel, at the urging of my son.

I swim deeper down, down through
the scale of evolutionary design to become
what I once was. Rubbery fins are now skin,
fingers are webbed. The water sustains me,
holds me forever in the present moment.

SEND IN THE CLONES

My daughters are strong women,
especially the eldest, my Pisces.

If you need help organizing your
life, resolving your crises,

call for the clones.
Who dubbed them clones?

An ex-husband, of course.
He is the source.

He saw they had minds of their own,
identities they would not disown.

Meekness is not in their bones.
He called them clones;

they didn't fit his idea, you see,
of what a woman should be.

After divorce he married a lass
who was quite willing to kiss his ass.

HEAVY EQUIPMENT

I take a last walk around their property to see the bushes and trees my son-in-law, a gifted gardener, has planted; sixteen years of his nurturing have brought them to artistic maturity. I stand on the spot where he put up an awning to soften the summer sun during family parties. I see my husband, in his white lawn chair, laughing, teasing children and grandchildren. Such a happy time! My nephew is here from Jackson. Katy and her family are up from Atlanta. The youngest grandchildren play in the sand and then run screeching into the cold lake. The older grandchildren sun themselves or nap in the hammock.

My eyes wander over to the empty spot the hot tub used to occupy, see my daughter and me sitting in it as she aims the jets of warm water onto my aching back in an effort to soothe me. I can't let her know how sad I am; no longer will I trespass across five neighbors' yards to get to her beach and wander up to the deck on a summer Saturday morning to share a cup of coffee, a quiet talk.

For the last time, I ascend the steps to the deck and look out at the lake to the spot where my husband died. She will no longer have to look there and be reminded of those agonizing minutes she and her husband stood watching as the emergency medical technicians tried to revive him. That memory is not the reason for the move. Son-in-law has heavy equipment, which he uses to supplement his retirement income. He has found property on another lake, far from complaining neighbors and barking dogs, a garage large enough to store his furniture-making tools and the family cars.

This morning my *heart* is heavy. I want something to remind me of the happiness of this place. A concrete turtle sits on the porch. I take it home.

MOTHER'S RORSCHACH

World War II is dragging on. Mother insists we pray for peace by saying the rosary each night. Tucked up in her blankets and pillows, she intones the first phrases of the Pater Nosters and Ave Marias while I kneel at the foot of her bed and try to stay alert enough to echo the responses.

She is devout but does one thing that is forbidden (only God can know the future). She tells my fortune by reading tea leaves. She brews the tea and pours it. I drink it and turn my cup over on its saucer. Mother rotates the cup three times. Carefully, she studies the shapes of leaves, which cling to the sides of the china. Excited, I listen to her describe people and events that might be part of my future. She cautions, *You must not take this seriously. It's just a game you and I are playing.*

I do not often feel close to my mother, but during our afternoons reading tea leaves and the nights we say the rosary, my need for closeness is fulfilled.

A MUTATION

It's 1938, and Mother and I are shopping for my Easter dress; she is searching one rack and I another. I run to her holding my choice, a powder blue organdy. *I want this one! No. You can't wear blue with those funny green eyes of yours. This yellow dress will look better on you.*

I go to the long mirror and peer up close at my eyes. Mother stands beside me. I can see our eyes are different. At home sitting around the dinner table, I notice my mother, dad, brother and sister all have fair skin and blue eyes. I look at my tanned arms, think about my green eyes and wonder, *Do I belong to this family?*

INTERLUDE

Hungry, late for a hair appointment,
I am parked outside the salon
and wolfing down a Big Mac.

Suddenly, I'm not there
or anywhere else.

Consciousness returns.
I've done it again: passed out
from a piece of food blocking my airway.

My neurologist says,
"Parkinson patients have difficulty swallowing;
take small bites, chew thoroughly."

I tell myself, *Be careful;*
one of these times
you might not come back.

Would that be so bad?
My interlude was peaceful.

AGE

A dried iris, past its prime, is taped
to a page in my journal. Wrinkled and
worn, I am still beautiful.

Some days I can barely walk, but today I *run*
clutching my puppy while a huge black dog
trots along the beach in our direction.

At Beaumont's Pain Clinic, my nurse
daughter says, "Mom doesn't need a
sedative. I'll talk her through the procedure."

I lie on my stomach while a physician
inserts a needle between my vertebrae.
My daughter chants, "Deep breathe, Mom."

Pain-free weeks will follow now, unless
I dance or garden too much,
or find a man to make love to me.

ELIXIR

A magic potion coats my emotions.
Real or imagined slights just slide off.
I move on. Nothing can hurt me.

I write because I must. It's survival.
I write because a part of me yearns
to connect, longs to have an impact.

Taking a risk would be dangerous. My magic
potion might fail me. A crack could develop in
my Teflon coat. My neediness might leak out.

Still, there is that yearning, but how can I reach
others when I have put up a shield?

My words are only words. Nothing is revealed.
They are as sounding brass, or a tinkling cymbal. *

*St. Paul's Letter to the Corinthians

*ALLONS**

Come all you poets!
Take me where I long to be,
outside myself into the beauty
of your world.

Age descends upon me.
I need the music of your words
to keep me from falling asleep.

Novels demand too much. I need your
brevity and rhythm, your vowel-laden words
that resound bell-like in my mind, then
drift into my heart where your meaning
becomes mine.

*French, *Arise*

OUR POETRY TEACHER

sprinkles ideas onto fertile soil
in our receptive minds.

Some have heads brimming with verse;
her ideas enhance what's already there.

Others need poetry perfume sprayed in class
before we can put words on paper.

She models a relaxed attitude:
If we love poetry, poetry will love us.

Her life is a poem.
She has a cat sitting on her head.

LOOKING OUT MY WINDOW

I am dew on the grass sparkling in morning sunshine
a peaceful lake imaging trees graceful on my banks
Mother Goose leading my young to feast on lavish grass
a blue iris multiplying myself tenfold against a white house
a wind sock, still now, having learned to be calm
sand on the beach eager for children's castles
a pear tree promising fruit after a spring full of blossoms
a wild cherry tree, tart from living, growing where I choose

RIPE RUSSETS

Like a pregnant woman about to give birth
our pear tree is heavily laden, limbs
awkward from the burden she carries.

Still, she is beautiful. Vivid red pears contrast
against green leaves. Her purpose: to nourish
all who reach for the fruit of her womb.

WAITING

Those Ladies in Waiting
to the Queen; what are
they waiting for?

I have been waiting all my life:
    waiting to grow up,
    waiting for my brother, my cousins,
    my boyfriend to come home from the service,
    waiting for my wedding,
    waiting for my babies to be born.

I waited for my children to be in school, so I could return to college.
I waited for job applications to be accepted, for promotions, for salary increases.
I waited for my retirement.

Now
    I wait for my car to be fixed, for sons, daughters and friends
    to take me to my appointments, for my tooth, back, and knees to stop
hurting.

I have spent too much of my life waiting, and I refuse to wait any longer.

IN THE MIDDLE OF THE NIGHT

I awaken with clenched fists
to a replay of yesterday's events
on my mind's movie screen.

While driving on a lonely road
I was rear-ended when I braked
for a squirrel. A large, angry man
got out of his car, banged on my

window and shouted, *You were
driving too slow, then braked
for no reason!* It took a long
time for the police to come.

Meditation will bring somnolence.
I focus on ceiling shadows,
cast by garden lights shining
through the trees.

A rumbling in my stomach
distracts me, brings back the
dream. I get up, tiptoe down the
hall to rummage in the fridge,

decide on a turkey sandwich
with pickles and mayonnaise.
Stuffing myself makes me feel
drowsy. Sleep will surely come.

It does.
Nightmares come with it.
I dream of World War III.

BROKEN MOMENT

On a Fourth of July morning in the year 2000, a woman stands by a quiet lake, absorbed in the beauty of her surroundings. The lake's reflection of powder blue sky, moist green leaves on trees moving in the breeze, warm sunshine, songs of the birds, all combine to soothe her senses.

Suddenly, she is jolted out of her reverie by the roar of two low-flying military jets. They fly in close formation, the fastest, loudest planes she has ever beheld. They spew their power across the sky.

Terrible and wonderful, they are gone as quickly as they have come.

The woman is pulled from her appreciation of the timeless beauty of nature and then thrust into the reality of the Twenty-First Century.

FINIS

The last apple on our tree
    clings to its branch,
        tenaciously.

Thunder storms in September
    do not sunder it
        from our tree.

A raccoon climbs,
    settles on a sturdy branch,
        plucks the last apple.

METAPHOR

In the beginning I followed directions.
Experience has taught me to do it my way.

I unwind each skein, begin to knit thoughtfully, meditating
about my relationships with others, with time and the universe.

Now, in a new phase with a new project, I realize that sooner or later
there will be no more yarn.

WRITING PROMPTS
AND REVISION EXERCISES

 **TRY THIS:**

What natural disaster or force of nature has touched your life? Write a list of the effects, giving specific details. Put yourself into that situation, even if it didn't happen to you. Read Mary Simion's *The Open Window* and *It Should Have Been Peter.* Also read Bernie DeHut's *Tagging the Serpent.*

Were you ever in a dangerous situation as a child? A near miss? What frightened you? Write down what you remember from the incident. Be specific. Try to include all the senses. What did you see? What colors? What sounds did you hear? Do you associate a taste with what happened? A touch? A feeling? Read Lori Goff's *Someone Watches Over Me* and Susan Kehoe's *Reflection on Spiders.* Also read Mary Simion's *Wolf at the Window.*

What bothers you about your job, your family, your day? Pick out the little things, the colors, the sounds, the feelings. Notice Polly Opsahl's *Postal Blues.* When she says, "I can't hold on any longer," she's talking about the letters she carries, but is she also talking about her life? Have you ever lost a job? What other job can you imagine yourself doing? How would you feel in this new job? Read Susan Kehoe's *Involuntary Separation.*

Pick three random objects from your junk drawer or walk outside and pick up items you see. Open your eyes wide and notice these as if seeing them for the first time. How do they relate to you? How do they relate to each other? Find a connection between them and yourself. Write it. Read *Sacred* by Polly Opsahl.

What secret do you have from your childhood that you've never told anyone? It can be a good secret or a not-so-good secret. Write it. How did you feel when it happened? How did you feel hiding it all this time? Remember colors, places, noises, people. Read Dinah Lee's *Not-So-Hot Pants* and Mary Simion's *Solfeggio.*

Think about your family members, both close and distant. Most families have someone who is a bit different. Perhaps that person has a physical or developmental struggle, has lived in a mental or criminal institution (or another confined setting). Perhaps his or her dress or behavior is eccentric or quirky. How have family gatherings incorporated this member into the activities? Is there an endearing characteristic about this person that you cherish? Is it difficult to balance shame, pride, embarrassment and love? Did this experience strengthen your patience, your balance in life, your direction? Write it. Read Dinah Lee's *The Watchdog Sleeps* and Susan Kehoe's *Crossing Forbidden Streets*. Also read Lori Goff's *Death in the Hills*.

How do you feel about your age? Make a list of things that are happening to you because of your age (i.e. acne, childbirth, menopause, wrinkles) and write your reactions. Read Maryhelen Hagood's *Metaphor, Age* and *Interlude*. Read Bob Simion's *Eyes* and Margo LaGattuta's *Trusting the Lake*.

Think of someone to whom you have something to say and have never done so. The person can be living or dead. Write a poem in a letter format (an epistle poem) telling that person what you've most wanted to say. Just write what you feel. Be honest; no one has to see it but you. Set it aside. In a day or two, go back to it and take out anything that's no longer important to you. Read Maryhelen Hagood's *Dear Beverly*.

Have you had a significant event happen in your life that has changed you in some way? How did you deal with it at the time? How are you dealing with it now? Has it changed your priorities? Do people treat you in a different way? Read Mary Ellen Soroka's *My Slow Changes,* Dinah Lee's *It All Began in the Closet*, Karen Marie Duquette's *Overcome By Silence* and Bernie DeHut's *Way to Go*.

What have you lost? How has that loss affected you? How did you deal with the various stages of loss? It could be a family member, a pet, a home, a job. Read Mary Ellen Soroka's *You Could Not Go Alone* and *Dad's Wireless Connection*. Also read Polly Opsahl's *ABC's of Friendship*, Maryhelen Hagood's *Anniversary Pictures*, Mary Simion's *Live Images* and Bernie DeHut's *Final Sale*.

What major historical event have you witnessed, either first-hand or through news stories? For example, it could be a war, the 9/11 attacks, the day President Kennedy, Princess Diana or Martin Luther King, Jr., died. Where were you when it happened? How did you feel: scared, angry, numb? How did this event affect your life? Write it. Read Bob Simion's *Night Drop* and *England—France 1943* and Mary Simion's *6 June 1944*.

Take an everyday occurrence in your life and list all the details. How did it affect you? How did it affect your family, others in your life? Write a story of these moments and how you feel about them. Read L. Marie Elsey's *The Secret of Life, A Celebration of the Bugflies,* and *The Fine Art of Fiddlin'.* Also read Bernie DeHut's *Answering the Call of the Wild.*

Can you remember an important teacher or mentor in your life? How did he or she affect you? Name one thing you heard that you never forgot. Read L. Marie Elsey's *Miss Vanalstine's 4th Grade Learning Extravaganza,* Maryhelen Hagood's *Our Poetry Teacher,* and Susan Kehoe's *Color Me Electric Aqua.*

A relationship between a parent or grandparent and child is powerful. Recall a close time with your parent, grandparent or child. Read Karen Marie Duquette's *In Praise of Roots,* Mary Ellen Soroka's *Mom Makes Pretty,* Bob Simion's *Crepes,* Polly Opsahl's *What Have I Done to My Daughter?,* Dinah Lee's *Bless Your Heart,* and Lori Goff's *Someone Watches Over Me.*

Sexuality plays an important role in each of our lives. Is there an event or relationship that has special meaning or is unresolved for you? Read Karen Duquette's *Her Place, Woman Marking Time* and *Becoming Fruit.* Also read Lori Goff's *Satin Sheets.*

Getting started with a life story means dealing with conflicting memories. That's because memory contains *emotions* and emotions always contain opposites, such as joy when graduating to something new while feeling sorrow when leaving other things behind. Writing about a happy moment and also remembering sad ones creates tension. But capturing the tension of opposites is what makes stories worth writing and worth reading.

Select one event that illustrates a significant experience. Write it in the middle of a page and draw a circle around it. Brainstorm all the words, images and phrases that come to mind branching out from that event and capturing them quickly on paper. This is a "messy" process because your mind will go in many directions, using both right and left-brain information. Notice that you recall an entire range of impressions, the bad as well as the good.

Finally, write a story that embraces all sides of the experience. Inconsistencies and conflicts don't necessarily need to be resolved. They can flesh out a story and make it more palpable. Sometimes a story is simply about the tension. Here is an example from Susan Kehoe's story, *A Day in the Park.*

Brainstorming example

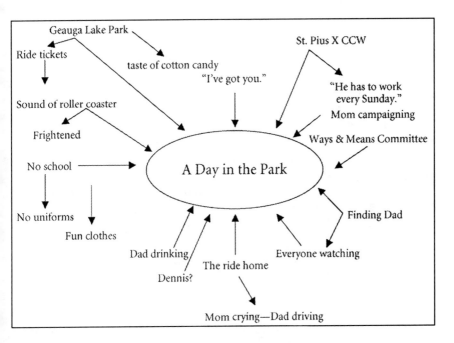

Poetry—What to Do After the Rejection, Revision Exercises
Margo LaGattuta

It is always a blow to the ego to have a poem you love rejected by an editor. However, after the initial disappointment, you have three choices:

1. Forget it, and never write again.
2. Assume it is just not right for that publisher, but send it elsewhere.
3. Begin the revision process, revise it, then send it out again.

If you choose option 1, you're out of the process, and you can count on never getting published. Option 2 might work. Try it and if, after three more tries, the poem is still rejected, you are ready for option 3. This one really works, if you're willing to work hard and study the craft of revision. Here are some approaches to revision (not necessarily to be done in this order …).

Revision Exercises

a. Does the poem need expansion? Does it have some wonderful images and beginnings, but ideas that are not developed fully enough for the reader to get involved? Make sure you don't leave out something crucial because it doesn't "fit" logically. If it feels connected (associatively), get it in the poem somehow.

b. Does the poem need shrinking? Did you go past a powerful ending and add just one or two more lines to say "Get it?" to the reader? Are there unnecessary opening lines, which you needed to get the poem started, but are no longer needed to enhance meaning?

c. Is the language lazy or ordinary? Have you used too many clichés or uninteresting nouns and verbs? Are there too many adjectives or adverbs? Remember, in poetry the ideas are much stronger with fewer distractions. Less is more (unless it's not enough!).

d. Notice line breaks. Does the poem read aloud well? Does it sound right if you take a breath where the line breaks? Are there all end-stopped lines, or do you vary them with enjambments? (Breaking the line between an adjective and a noun, for example.) Does the poem sound better written in prose (without selected line breaks)?

e. Are there rewards for the reader? Does the poem grab his/her attention with power right away? Could the parts (lines, stanzas) be rearranged to make the order more interesting, or more logical? Does the ending leave the reader with an epiphany? Or a letdown?

f. Look at the voice. Does it talk down to the reader, or make him/her feel dumb or lectured? Remember, if the voice endears itself to the reader, you're ahead!

g. Is the poem universal? Remember, we not only want to tell *our* story (the reader, unless she's our mother, might not care)—we want the reader to find his/her own story in it. Metaphor is a wonderful technique for this.

h. Is the poem sentimental or emotional? Sentiment doesn't move the reader. It usually just moves the writer. The reader needs to *feel* the emotion—not be told. Often a poem is sentimental if it doesn't deal with enough tension of opposites. Emotions are not just black or white. They're more complex (good can be bad, etc.). Oxymoron works well for this.

i. What is the emotional context of the poem? Do you know something you don't want to tell the reader? Is there some information you could add that would illuminate the meaning somehow?

j. If the poem is in the first person, try it in the second or third person.

k. Do you need some logical connective threads or can you remove some— so the mind has to leap from part to part in the poem?

Prose—Tips for Creating and Editing Stories
Margo LaGattuta

a. Aim for an attention-grabber opening. Remember that most readers read only until they get bored, so make your opening surprising and mysterious, so that readers will want to know what's going to happen next.

b. Place your story in a landscape. Let your readers know rather quickly into the action where this scene takes place and how this landscape will play into the content of the story.

c. Create lively characters. Use realistic dialogue and lots of specific descriptions to allow your characters to come to life in the reader's imagination.

d. Make sure your story has creative tension. Most stories begin when something goes wrong and there is a problem to solve.

e. The old familiar cliché "show, don't tell" stills works to make powerful, engaging stories. Don't tell the readers how to feel. Create scenes and events that help them to experience situations first-hand.

f. Think about verbs. They are the action of your stories. Make them original and descriptive. Avoid using a lot of "to be" verbs and passive voice constructions (verbs that have the subject *receiving* the action rather than *doing* the action, like "The tickets were hidden by Jim," which would be better as "Jim hid the tickets"). Try using present tense verbs to bring the action of your story alive in the current moment. Memories and dream sequences are especially powerful in the present tense.

g. Use lots of nouns and specific details, rather than general ones (for example, "a rusty Ford jalopy" instead of "a car"). Use a journal to gather interesting names of places, towns, and people to use in your stories.

h. Pare back repetitions and tendencies to over-tell concepts. Trust your readers to read into your images, dialogues, actions and descriptions for content.

i. In creative nonfiction (or memoir) use reflections to enhance your stories. Give readers some insights about your inner thoughts and revelations. Tell what you learned from this experience or how it changed you.

j. Pay attention to ambivalence (people having opposite or conflicting emotions simultaneously). Let your characters be complex and embrace contraries.

k. Open the door to wonder and mystery. Suggest meaning with figurative language (metaphor, simile, alliteration, etc.) and allow your readers to find undercurrents on their own.

l. Write stories about things you don't understand. Allow the creative process to reveal truths to you while you're revealing them to readers. If you start with an agenda for giving the readers profound insights, your story may come off as preachy and turn readers off instead of engaging them in discoveries.

m. Go for the hard place. Write about situations you've never revealed to anyone or secrets you're embarrassed to expose. Most readers will relate and respect your honesty.

n. Have fun with words. Use delicious words that are fun to say and will enhance readers' enjoyment of sound and rhythm. Poetic language works well in prose as well as in poetry.

o. If your story is plot-driven, lead toward a climax or turn-around event, a place where your tale has a surprising revelation—before it reaches the *denouement,* outcome or resolution. Sometimes this is called the *arc* of the story.

p. Avoid endings that tie everything up with a bow. Life is more complicated than that. Hollywood endings make readers wince and make your stories less realistic.

ABOUT THE WRITERS

Margo LaGattuta, 2005 winner of The Mark Twain Award for her contribution to Midwestern Literature, has her MFA from Vermont College and four published collections of poetry. Her poetry and essays have appeared in many national literary magazines and anthologies, including *The MacGuffin, The Cincinnati Poetry Review, Negative Capability, Woman Poet Midwest* and *Yankee Magazine.* She has done writer-in-the-schools residencies and teacher in-service sessions, both locally and nationally, for 20 years and edited eight anthologies for small presses. In 2002/2003 she received a Michigan Creative Artist's Grant from ArtServe Michigan to complete her newest poetry collection. Margo writes for *Suburban Lifestyles* in Rochester, where she creates a weekly creative nonfiction column, articles and theater reviews. She teaches writing at the University of Michigan and other schools and conducts creative writing workshops.

L. Marie Elsey is a wife, mother, grandmother, storywriter, political activist, and an old hippie. Her stories and articles have appeared in the *Royal Oak Tribune, Detroit Free Press, USA Today,* Wayne State University's *South End,* and Mercy Bellbrook's *Bits and Pieces.* In college a professor asked her, "Do you know you have writing talent?" It took forty years and this collaboration for her to realize he was right.

Mary Ellen Soroka was born in Youngstown, Ohio. She earned her Bachelors degree in social work from Eastern Michigan University. In her former life, she was a social worker in the field of gerontology. She served on the Planning Commission in her community, was president of the local historical society and maintains an interest in local politics. She's a member of Zeta Tau Alpha, Springfed Arts—Metro Detroit Writers, and the Poetry Society of Michigan. Mary Ellen enjoys painting with pastels and taking long walks with her dog. She's lived in Michigan for twenty-four years with her husband and began her commitment to writing after a head injury.

Bob Simion has had many adventures. After serving in World War II with the Office of Strategic Services (O.S.S.), the forerunner of the C.I.A., he returned to the states and studied at the University of Detroit and graduated with two degrees, a BS in Foreign Trade and an MBA. He then joined the corporate world and retired from banking after forty-six years. During this time he did some procedural and technical writing. He started writing for himself, his family and others who expressed interest in his life experiences. In 2000, his wife Mary and he began attending writing workshops to improve their skills. They continue attending and writing. He is a member of Springfed Arts—Metro Detroit Writers, Poetry Society of Michigan, The American Legion, Delta Phi Epsilon and ISAR, the International Society of Astrological Research.

Susan Kehoe has a PhD in cognitive psychology and education, which she applies as a consultant in corporate America. Susan is past president of Cranbrook Writers' Guild. She has taught business and technical writing at the University of Michigan and Wayne State University, but her real love is writing fiction and memoir. She is currently completing a book of memoirs, some of which are featured in this anthology. Susan is an avid reader who enjoys digital photography and scrapbooking. She lives in Bloomfield Hills, Michigan, with her husband and dog.

Polly Opsahl is a letter carrier, union activist and award-winning poet. She lives in Rochester Hills, Michigan, with her husband and daughter. She has been published in two anthologies, *Almost Touching* and *Everywhere is Someplace Else,* and several literary publications. Polly is a member of the Poetry Society of Michigan, the National Federation of State Poetry Societies, and Detroit Working Writers. She has a book manuscript entered in publication contests.

Bernie DeHut spent most of her business career in corporate management, working in the U.S. and Europe. Motorcycle touring was her passion away from the office; she visited forty-nine states and most Canadian provinces as either passenger or driver. She's recently relocated to Michigan's Upper Peninsula where she's working on her next career, nonfiction writing, with the assistance of her cats. She was named a finalist in Gather.com's 2006 Travel Writing contest.

Karen Marie Duquette is a problem-solver by nature. She has a Bachelor of Social Work degree from Western Michigan University and an advanced degree from the school of hard knocks—Post Traumatic Stress Disorder—formed by her job at Social Security, where she spent twenty years, her first working life, adjudicating disability claims. Also a union activist while there, she negotiated state employees' first labor contracts under civil service rules. In 2000, she erupted into poetry while helping a published poet obtain her disability benefits, and one writing road led to another. She is in the midst of writing novels while poems just pile up. Words have become her passion, and now she is giving voice to the voiceless, telling trauma stories for those who can't yet speak. She lives in Okemos, Michigan, with her husband, Jay, who inspires the romance writer in her.

Mary Simion started secretly writing stories in her closet as a child. She also practiced the piano incessantly and has a degree in music. She has been a certified astrologer for twenty-six years. She is married to Bob, who is also in this book. She has one brother. She is the mother of four, grandmother of seven, great-grandmother of seven, aunt of seven, great-aunt of fourteen. She is foster mother of two cats, Poochie and Annie. Sometimes, she thinks of her poems as children of the mind produced by the heart. She enjoys gardening and grows flowers and vegetables. She is a member of ISAR (International Society for Astrological Research), the Poetry Society of Michigan, and Springfed Arts—Metro Detroit Writers.

Lori Goff, in another lifetime, scribbled in a diary, tried her hand at songwriting, and kept a log of trips. Some writings she did for a reason and others in a season of inspiration. Scraps of paper, matchbook covers, napkins, and bills, whatever was handy she used to capture a magic moment of thought. After a career spanning over four decades in the airline industry, she writes for a second chance to polish those early efforts. *The Heart of It All,* (iUniverse), her book of poetry and prose, was published in 2006. Previously published works appeared in *Ridgewriters, Woods-N-Water News* and other journals.

Dinah Lee has always been a storyteller at heart. Uncertain of the reaction to her work, she used to keep the stories to herself. With the hope of helping others through knowledge and understanding, she now shares them. Dinah has a degree in Psychology and Criminal Justice and has spent most of her career in corporate management. She is happily married and lives in the country with a big red dog, two cats, a stone fire pit, and a flower garden. Dinah enjoys camping, reading, gardening, trying new recipes, and surrounding herself with humorous friends. She is always working on the next story.

Maryhelen Hagood has an MA in Guidance and Counseling from Oakland University, having returned to college when her children were in school. She has worked as an adult education teacher, a counselor for the MOST program (Michigan Occupational and Skills Training), a guidance counselor at an alternative high school and a counselor in a shelter for victims of domestic violence. She started writing at age seventy.

978-0-595-42727-7
0-595-42727-8

Printed in the United States
78431LV00004B/232-255

9 780595 427277